Variations on a T

QUILTS WITH EASY OPTI

TERRY MARTIN

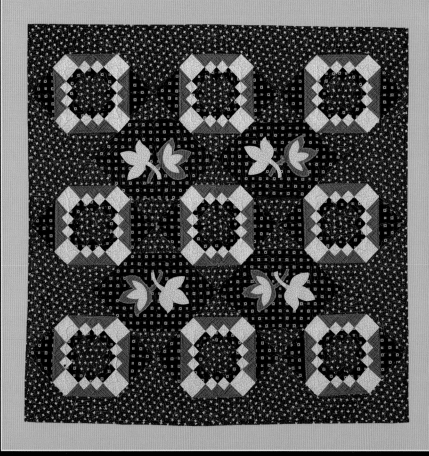

Martingale®
& C O M P A N Y

Variations on a Theme: Quilts with Easy Options
© 2006 Terry Martin

That Patchwork Place® is an imprint of
Martingale & Company®.

Martingale & Company
20205 144th Avenue NE
Woodinville, WA 98072-8478
www.martingale-pub.com

CREDITS

President: **Nancy J. Martin**
CEO: **Daniel J. Martin**
COO: **Tom Wierzbicki**
Publisher: **Jane Hamada**
Editorial Director: **Mary V. Green**
Managing Editor: **Tina Cook**
Technical Editor: **Darra Williamson**
Copy Editor: **Melissa Bryan**
Design Director: **Stan Green**
Illustrator: **Robin Strobel**
Cover and Text Designer: **Stan Green**
Photographer: **Brent Kane**

MISSION STATEMENT

Dedicated to providing quality products and
service to inspire creativity.

DEDICATION

To all of you wonderfully talented quilters
with a passion for fabric, a good sense of
humor, the desire to have fun, and the
need to create. And to you, Cornelia, my
best friend: we laugh until we cry.

Printed in China
11 10 09 08 07 06   8 7 6 5 4 3 2 1

Library of Congress Cataloging-in-Publication Data
Library of Congress Control Number: 2006002327

ISBN-13 : 978-1-56477-671-6
ISBN-10 : 1-56477-671-9

Contents

Preface

I love to sew quilts. It's part of my everyday life, and I thank my family for understanding that. I love poring over books of quilting blocks looking for inspiration. I even dream about designing quilts in my sleep.

The collection of quilts in this book came from a challenge I gave myself. I was astounded by the variety of novelty prints I'm attracted to in quilt shops and by the extensive selection already in my stash. So I set this goal: to produce a book in which all the quilts include novelty prints in one form or another. Off to work I went! I hope you enjoy making these quilts as much as I did.

For a creative adventure, I encourage you to make these quilts your own. Look at each quilt from your point of view—consider your color palette and how you would change the design to make it better, different, yours. I want these quilt projects to spark your creativity and make ideas race around in your head the way they race around in mine. I believe quilting is a wonderful, addictive outlet for the creative soul, and I want to spread the addiction to everyone!

But sometimes I get stumped; I don't know what to do with a fabric selection, how treat a border, or—especially—when to call a project complete. This is where my quilting buddies come in. For years I was a closet quilter. I taught myself, looked at a couple of books, saw some terrific quilts at shows, and quietly made quilts in my own little bubble. Some were good, some were okay, and some were . . . yikes! I found that quilting in my bubble was safe but not very satisfying, and then I discovered the joy of quilting with friends.

I joined a quilt guild and kept a low profile while I soaked up lots of ideas. I rediscovered old friends that had begun quilting years before I did, and I dragged my best friend and a sister into the quilting world. I couldn't be happier now. Anytime I'm stuck, my friends come to the rescue with a simple suggestion, like "That border needs rickrack," or "Put the whole thing on point and see what it does to the block," or "A pieced border would tie everything together." With these quick suggestions and the tossing in and out of fabric possibilities, I am off to work again in total bliss, eager to complete the project.

So I recommend that you stretch your creativity, make these projects yours, and seek friendship in quilting. I'm not saying that quilting will cure all, but I do know that the camaraderie—along with that fat quarter you recently picked up at your quilt shop that's just perfect for the quilt you're working on—can certainly help!

Introduction

Novelty prints are my thing. They make me smile!

When I started quilting and collecting cotton fabrics for quilts, I was always drawn to novelty prints. What can be more fun than butterflies floating across a blue sky, fabulous cherries in every color and size, Halloween pumpkins grinning back at you, or green and red holly prints that ring in the Yule tidings? I love novelty prints: they add meaning, memories, passion, and decoration to my life and to my quilts.

And I think there is a little magic in novelty prints. Make a sports-themed quilt for your hubby and he'll quit asking if you have enough fabric after bringing in the umpteenth bag from the quilt shop. Make a rubber ducky quilt for the little one and he will love rubber duckies for the rest of his life (see hubby). Make a kitchen table topper wild with cherry fabrics of all kinds, and—how fabulous!—it matches perfectly with the cherry-decorated dishes. It's all good!

Now, if you're a collector like I am, you'll have your stash of novelty prints tucked away, not quite sure what to do with them. This book is for you! And for those of you who love novelty prints but never buy them because they're just a little too intimidating to work with, especially with their larger motifs, brighter colors, and directional designs—well, this book is for you too!

I will show you how to develop confidence when planning a quilt that includes anywhere from 1 to 20 different novelty prints. I will share my tips for quilting with novelty prints and warn you about the pitfalls I've encountered, so you can avoid them. I've also designed all the projects to work well with a variety of novelty prints.

For those of you who are still a little shy when working with novelty prints and just can't imagine the patterns in more traditional fabric, I've re-created each quilt using more traditional fabrics and a wide variety of colorways for you to compare and contrast. The alternate projects are simple to create using the blocks from the original patterns. In most cases, I've also used different settings to show how the blocks can be used in different ways. Some of the alternate looks result in quilts that are larger than the original project, but most are smaller versions. I hope this will stretch your quilting talents and allow you to see all the possibilities these projects can offer.

I invite you to come play with me and with all the fabulous novelty prints that you see and would love to work with. I've always loved to see what quilters have done with my designs, especially how they've interpreted them using their own fabric choices!

Happy Quilting!

Terry Martin

Novelty Prints and How to Use Them

What is considered a novelty, conversation, or theme print? All these labels describe the same thing, with one small exception. Unlike novelty or conversation prints, I think theme-printed fabric can be a little more subtle—perhaps even a smaller-scale print.

I consider a novelty print any fabric that uses a recognizable character or object as a motif. For instance (this list could go on forever so I'm naming only the ones that pop into my head this very moment; I'm sure you can think of many more!):

- Cats and dogs (animal motifs)
- Oranges, apples, and pears (fruit motifs)
- Booties, rattles, and snuggly bears (baby-related motifs)
- Flip-flops and umbrellas (beach motifs)
- Santas, elves, and lights (Christmas motifs)
- Baseballs and basketballs (sports motifs)
- And don't forget those wonderful plastic pink flamingos and other kitschy icons!

Novelty prints make me smile, laugh, ooh and aah, remember, and wish for a baby to snuggle. These prints are so much fun to quilt with.

Novelty prints come in all shapes, sizes, and colors. Almost every quilt shop carries novelty prints in one form or another, especially in the section with baby or children's fabrics. The thing I love best about novelty prints is that they evoke emotion: they are meaningful and bring back memories. When making a quilt for a loved one, isn't it fabulous to think of that person and what they love in life? My daughter, at just over six feet tall, used to be quite the basketball player, and adding her jersey number and her school's initial to a quilt created with basketball fabric made the perfect gift. I can't tell you how proud I am of that lap-sized quilt, especially when she pulled it out of her sports bag and all her teammates "oohed" and "aahed."

I found a reproduction print in the quilt shop the other day that was the exact same print my grandmother used for curtains in her kitchen. I bought three yards.

And what is it about pink flamingos? I see them everywhere, from goofy lawn ornaments to subtle prints in home-decorating fabric. The pink flamingo print in the quilt shown on page 26 made me laugh. I bought four yards of that fabric.

I've made two sports quilts for my husband, and matching curtains for his den. He's a happy guy.

A friend of mine made a set of pillow-cases for her sister from a novelty print that featured seductive outdoor girls wearing plaid; her sister loved them because she is an outdoorsy kind of gal.

And the "sickness" goes on, luckily with no cure in sight! So do the fun, joy, memories, and happy times using novelty prints in the quilting you do for yourself and for others.

CHOOSING AND USING NOVELTY FABRICS

Now let's talk about the advantages in using novelty prints and just a couple of things to watch out for. When I'm designing quilts, I work from one of two different angles. Either I find the block and setting I'd like to use and then select the fabric, or I find the fabric and then design a pattern to fit it. Either way works, but it's almost easier for me to let the fabric "do the talking."

Although I am able to hand and machine quilt, I'd rather be creating new designs and piecing them together than quilting them. I'm hoping someday my creativity will extend into quilting, but until then, I surround myself with fabulous machine quilters and novelty prints! Because novelty prints—by their nature—are motif-specific, and the print is generally large in scale, fancy quilting, whether done by machine or by hand, is easily lost in the fabric. As a result, I'm able to use simple utilitarian quilting designs and techniques to tie the quilt sandwich together. This way the fabric takes the spotlight.

When I'm working with novelty prints, I look for (or design) blocks that show off the fabric, and I tend to work with blocks that include large open areas. More open space means fewer pieces and less piecing—see where I'm going? Less piecing allows me to show off the novelty print and make larger blocks, enabling me to make larger quilts quickly. Quick-and-easy patterns are a great way to play with novelty prints! How fabulous is that?

WARNING: There are a few things to keep in mind when working with novelty prints. The first is the scale of the print, because the scale of the typical novelty print is usually larger than that of most other prints. As I've already mentioned, there are advantages in using a fabric with a larger-scale print, but you must also consider that cutting up the print too much destroys its imagery and its impact; the motif becomes lost in the block and in the quilt. Limit the novelty print to the wide-open spaces of your block unless the scale is more moderate and workable in smaller spaces.

To preview how my choices will work, I generally make up a test block, and believe me, at times this step has saved both the quilt and my sanity. If I work up a test block and it doesn't "look right," I can make the necessary adjustments in my fabric choices before proceeding. I'm much happier making these simple changes at the beginning of a project than I would be cutting fabric for all 20 blocks and then finding out the fabrics are struggling to be recognized. This saves time and fabric and determines whether or not I will be fit to live with for the next couple of hours!

The other consideration when working with novelty prints is that often they are directional. Directional fabric is fabric with a motif best viewed from a specific direction and that doesn't "read" correctly when viewed from a different angle. Unless you mean for the cow on the fabric to be floating giddily upside down, you'll need to be a little careful when placing a directional print.

I used directional fabric for several quilts in this book, and since I pulled most of the fabrics from my stash, I was limited to the yardage I had on hand. In the quilt on page 21, I had enough fabric to cut the borders lengthwise so that all the rubber duckies faced the "right" way. But sometimes I had to turn the fabric in different directions because I didn't have enough fabric to run it all in one direction. There are various ways to work around this problem. Ask yourself how the quilt is going to be used. Will it be a wall hanging or a table topper? Will it be thrown over the couch or dragged around by a toddler? If it's a wall hanging, try to orient the directional fabric consistently facing one way or at

These blocks with the open center really get my imagination going. What can I stick in there next?!

Directional fabric can be a little tricky to work with, but with a little forethought they are just too much fun to use!

least facing inward toward the quilt center. Take a look at the "Garden Party" alternate quilt on page 55. I didn't have enough of the large-scale pumpkin fabric to cut it so that all the pumpkins faced one way in the border. Because I might hang this quilt, I arranged the pumpkins facing inward. The viewer's eye is directed subtly toward the center of the quilt instead of wandering off in various directions.

If, however, you're planning to use the quilt as a table topper, you'll need to orient the fabric as you want it to look for guests sitting around or looking down at the table. If the quilt hangs over the table, how should the directional fabric run? Will it be OK if the pink flamingos are flying upside down? Take a moment when gathering your fabrics to ask yourself what the quilt will be used for and how you'll want to orient the novelty print.

While you're piecing the blocks together, lay them all out in rows facing the way you want them. There's nothing more frustrating than having to pick out a row because the center block is sideways or upside down, an experience I can relate to—a couple of times!

OK, we've picked a pattern, found the perfect fabrics, anticipated the joy of working with novelty prints, and become aware of some pitfalls—let's get busy!

Cinco de Mayo

Made and quilted by Terry Martin, Snohomish, Washington. This quilt makes a great table topper, especially when celebrating the festive holiday Cinco de Mayo. Cover it with a heavy piece of plastic from the fabric store to prevent the guacamole dip from staining!

Have I told you I have a compulsion to coordinate projects a little too much? The name of the block in this quilt is Mexican Star—a pretty block I hadn't seen worked up into a quilt lately. Naturally I reached for my Southwestern-themed fabric: the chili-pepper print was just perfect. Olé!

At first this block looked a little intimidating, but once I broke it down into its parts, it was fun to put together. Please note that once the blocks are squared, the corners will be cut on the bias, so take care in pressing to make sure the block doesn't twist out of shape.

Finished Quilt: 39⅝" x 39⅝" ～ **Finished Block:** 14" x 14"

MATERIALS

All yardages are based on 42"-wide fabric.

1½ yards of red bandana print for blocks and setting triangles

1⅛ yards of blue chili-pepper print for blocks and binding

⅝ yard of bright yellow tone-on-tone print for blocks

2½ yards of fabric for backing*

44" x 44" piece of batting

*If your fabric measures a full 44" wide after it's been laundered, you'll need only 1⅓ yards of backing fabric.

CUTTING

All measurements include ¼"-wide seam allowances. Cut all strips across the width of the fabric (selvage to selvage).

From the blue chili-pepper print, cut:

- 2 strips, 3⅞" x 42"; crosscut into 20 squares, 3⅞" x 3⅞". Cut each square once diagonally to yield 2 half-square triangles (40 total).
- 2 strips, 2⅝" x 42"; crosscut into 20 squares, 2⅝" x 2⅝"
- 1 strip, 7¼" x 42"; crosscut into 5 squares, 7¼" x 7¼". Cut each square twice diagonally to yield 4 quarter-square triangles (20 total).
- 1 square, 2" x 2"
- 5 strips, 2½" x 42", for binding

From the bright yellow tone-on-tone print, cut:

- 4 strips, 2⅝" x 42"; crosscut into 32 rectangles, 2⅝" x 4¾"
- 2 strips, 2" x 42"; crosscut into:
    4 rectangles, 2" x 10"
    4 squares, 2" x 2"

From the red bandana print, cut:

- 1 strip, 2⅝" x 42"; crosscut into 8 rectangles, 2⅝" x 4¾"
- 5 strips, 2" x 42"; crosscut into 16 rectangles, 2" x 10"
- 1 square, 21⅛" x 21⅛"; cut twice diagonally to yield 4 quarter-square triangles
- 1 strip, 10⅞" x 42"; crosscut into 2 squares, 10⅞" x 10⅞". Cut each square once diagonally to yield 2 half-square triangles (4 total).

Making the Blocks

You'll make five blocks for this quilt: four in one colorway for the corner blocks (block A) and one in a different colorway for the center block (block B).

1. Sew a blue half-square triangle to a 2⅝" x 4¾" yellow rectangle as shown. Trim the excess fabric, leaving a ¼"-wide seam allowance; press. Make 16 of each.

Make 16 of each.

2. Repeat step 1 using the remaining blue half-square triangles and the 2⅝" x 4¾" red rectangles. Make four of each.

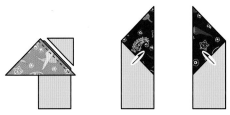

Make 4 of each.

3. Sew a 2⅝" blue square to 16 identical units from step 1 as shown; press.

Make 16.

4. Sew a blue quarter-square triangle to the remaining 16 units as shown; press.

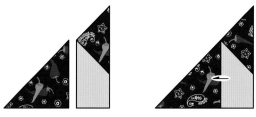

Make 16.

5. Repeat steps 3 and 4, using the units from step 2, the remaining 2⅝" blue squares, and the remaining blue quarter-square triangles. Make four of each.

Make 4.

Make 4.

6. Sew together one of each type of unit from steps 3 and 4 as shown; press. Make 16.

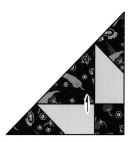

Make 16.

7. Repeat step 6 using the units from step 5. Make four.

Make 4.

8. Sew a 2" x 10" red rectangle between two units from step 6; press. Make sure one short end of the rectangle is aligned with the bottom edge of the unit as shown. Make eight.

Make 8.

9. Repeat step 8 using the units from step 7 and the 2" x 10" yellow rectangles. Make two.

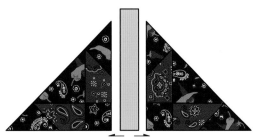

Make 2.

10. Sew a 2" yellow square between two remaining 2" x 10" red rectangles as shown; press. Make four. Sew each unit between two units from step 8. Press, square up the blocks to measure 14½" x 14½", and label these block A.

Make 4.

14½"

Block A.
Make 4.

continued on page 16

"CINCO DE MAYO" ALTERNATE

Whether worked up in Southwestern prints or cool batiks, the Mexican Star is a versatile block with lots of pizzazz.

A funny thing happened when I used these cool colors and rich, deep batiks for "Cinco de Mayo." When I set the blocks in vertical and horizontal rows, rather than on point, all I could see was a huge X across the face of the quilt top. I couldn't see anything else of the block—yikes! By adding a small setting strip between the blocks, I calmed things down quite a bit and let the block really show its stuff.

I love to play with settings for blocks when they don't work on their own. Sometimes—as in this example—using a simple frame for a block really does the trick.

11. Repeat step 10 using the 2" blue square and the remaining 2" x 10" yellow rectangles. Press, square up the block to measure 14½" x 14½", and label this block B.

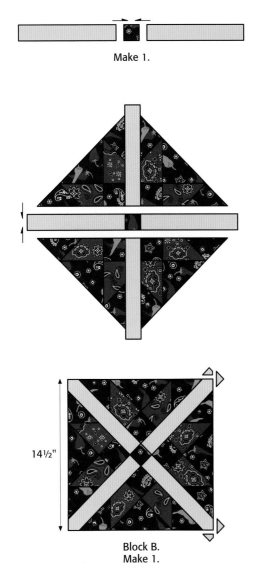

Make 1.

14½"

Block B.
Make 1.

ASSEMBLING THE QUILT

Refer to the assembly diagram at upper right and arrange the blocks, red quarter-square side setting triangles, and red half-square corner setting triangles in diagonal rows. Sew the blocks and side setting triangles into rows; press. Sew the rows together, adding the corner triangles last; press. Square up the quilt, making sure to maintain a ¼"-wide seam allowance around the edges.

Assembly diagram

FINISHING THE QUILT

Refer to "Finishing" on pages 76–79 as needed to complete the following steps.

1. Layer the quilt top with the batting and backing. Baste the layers together.

2. Hand or machine quilt as desired. I like to manipulate the decorative stitches on my sewing machine by increasing the stitch width or length. This adds a unique look to the quilt top without a lot of work. On this quilt, I lengthened the multiple-stitch zigzag (or mending) stitch to give the quilt top a controlled wavy line of quilting.

3. Square up the quilt sandwich. Add a hanging sleeve if desired.

4. Using the 2½" x 42" blue strips, make the binding and finish the edges of the quilt. Add a label if desired.

Vintage Flutterbys

Made by Terry Martin, Snohomish, Washington. Quilted by Becky Marshall. One of my guild members is crazy about butterflies. I'll have to watch that this quilt doesn't "fly away" when I show it at the next guild meeting!

The Robert Kaufman fabric company sent me a bit of each of their latest Little Darlings 1930s prints and I had a lot of fun using them in this quilt. Novelty prints can be very versatile, in this case giving each Flutterby block a different character depending on which prints I chose.

As I've mentioned before, novelty prints evoke memories for me. When I was working with this fabric I remembered that I used to give my daughter butterfly kisses on her cheeks as part of our good-night ritual when she was a little girl. She is now 18 and when I reminded her of those long-ago kisses, she gave me one!

Although I used a variety of colors, wouldn't this quilt be cute done all in pinks for a little girl's room?

Finished Quilt: 55" x 55" ~~⟲ **Finished Block: 9" x 9"**

MATERIALS

All yardages are based on 42"-wide fabric unless otherwise noted.

1⅞ yards *total* of scraps or fat eighths of assorted 1930s reproduction prints for blocks★

1½ yards *total* of scraps or fat eighths of 8 different solids and prints for block sashing★★

⅞ yards of white tone-on-tone print for blocks

⅜ yard of dark brown print for blocks

⅝ yard of blue 1930s reproduction print for binding

3⅓ yards of fabric for backing

60" x 60" piece of batting

★I used 10 blues, 7 greens, 4 purples, 3 reds, 5 pinks, and 2 oranges. Please feel free to substitute your own favorite color combinations.

★★I used equal amounts of red, yellow, orange, green, blue, yellow, and pink solids, and 1 lavender print.

CUTTING

All measurements include ¼"-wide seam allowances. Cut all strips across the width of the fabric (selvage to selvage).

From the white tone-on-tone print, cut:

- 5 strips, 2" x 42"; crosscut into 100 squares, 2" x 2"
- 3 strips, 1" x 42"; crosscut into 100 squares, 1" x 1"
- 7 strips, 1½" x 42"; crosscut into 25 rectangles, 1½" x 9½"

From the assorted 1930s reproduction prints, cut:

- 100 rectangles, 4½" x 5", in matching sets of 2

From the dark brown print, cut:

- 5 strips, 1½" x 42"; crosscut into 25 rectangles, 1½" x 6"

From the assorted solids and prints,
cut a *total* of:

- 50 rectangles, 1½" x 9½"
- 50 rectangles, 1½" x 11½"

From the blue 1930s reproduction print, cut:

- 6 strips, 2½" x 42"

MAKING THE BLOCKS

You'll make 25 Flutterby blocks for this quilt.

1. Referring to "Folded-Corner Piecing" on page 74 as needed, sew a 2" white square and a 1" white square to opposite corners of each 4½" x 5" reproduction print rectangle as shown. Trim the excess fabric, leaving a ¼"-wide seam allowance; press. Make 50 of each in fabric-matched sets of two.

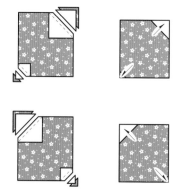

Make 50 of each
(in fabric-matched pairs).

2. Working next to your sewing machine, arrange two pairs of fabric-matched units (four units total) from step 1 to create the butterfly wings. Sew the units together as shown; press. Make 50 of each.

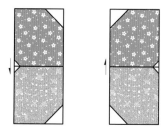

Make 50 of each.

3. Fold the corners of each 1½" x 6" brown rectangle to the wrong side to make a point at both ends as shown; press. Make 25. Don't worry if your points are not identical; no two butterflies are identical in nature.

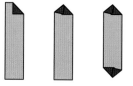

Make 25.

4. Center a unit from step 3 over each 1½" x 9½" white rectangle and pin in place as shown. Make 25.

Make 25.

5. Sew each unit from step 4 between two fabric-matched units from step 2 as shown; press. Make 25.

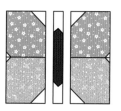

Make 25.

6. Randomly select and sew two 1½" x 9½" assorted solid or print rectangles to the sides of each unit from step 5; press. Repeat to sew 1½" x 11½" solid or print rectangles to the top and bottom of each unit; press. Make 25.

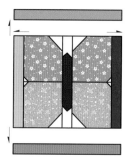

Make 25.

ASSEMBLING THE QUILT

Refer to the assembly diagram below and arrange the blocks in five horizontal rows of five blocks each, mixing the colors as much as possible. Sew the blocks into rows; press. Sew the rows together; press.

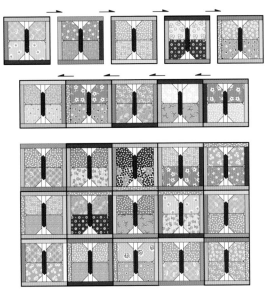

Assembly diagram

FINISHING THE QUILT

Refer to "Finishing" on pages 76–79 as needed to complete the following steps.

1. Layer the quilt top with the batting and backing. Baste the layers together.

2. Hand or machine quilt as desired. Becky Marshall had fun enhancing the wings of my Flutterby blocks. Sometimes simple quilting brings out the best in the fabrics!

3. Square up the quilt sandwich. Add a hanging sleeve if desired.

4. Using the 2½" x 42" blue strips, make the binding and finish the edges of the quilt. Add a label if desired.

"VINTAGE FLUTTERBYS" ALTERNATE

In this version of "Flutterbys," I started with the butterfly print fabric I chose for the border, but then I was having a hard time picking the right fabrics for the blocks. I wanted to use mostly batiks because of their swirling colors and liquid look, but was getting nowhere. My best friend, Cornelia, came over and by the time I fetched sodas for us, she had picked out all the fabrics! Don't you just love best friends?

Machine quilting makes this quilt finish quickly! I quilted concentric ovals over the wings, using decorative thread to match, and I used simple, straight-line quilting on the alternate blocks.

Rubber Duckies

Made by Terry Martin, Snohomish, Washington. Quilted by Becky Marshall. Who knew you could put bright red and teal together without them fighting each other for dominance?

This rubber ducky fabric is the cutest thing I've seen! Even the bubbles floating on the water have an iridescence.

A lot of adults are just big kids at heart. Take for example my husband, Ed. He has a small rubber duck collection and is always on the lookout for an interesting addition. One of his prize rubber ducks is a devil duck with horns!

This block lends itself to a number of different fabric collections, especially the larger-scale novelty prints. I've designated enough fabric to accommodate a one-way fabric design as shown in the border of my quilt. We can't have rubber ducks swimming sideways!

Finished Quilt: 48" x 60"   **Finished Block:** 12" x 12"

MATERIALS

All yardages are based on 42"-wide fabric, unless otherwise noted.

2⅝ yards of rubber duck print for blocks, outer border, and binding
¾ yard of orange print for blocks
¾ yard of teal tone-on-tone print for blocks
⅝ yard of yellow star print for blocks and inner border
⅜ yard of red print for blocks
3 yards of fabric for backing (horizontal seam)
54" x 66" piece of batting

CUTTING

All measurements include ¼"-wide seam allowances. Cut all strips across the width of the fabric (selvage to selvage) unless instructed otherwise.

From each of the orange and teal prints, cut:
- 10 strips, 2" x 42"; crosscut into:
  24 rectangles, 2" x 6½" (48 total)
  24 rectangles, 2" x 9½" (48 total)

From the *lengthwise* grain of the rubber duck print, cut:
- 2 strips, 5½" x 60½"

From the remaining rubber duck print, cut:
- 12 squares, 6½" x 6½"
- 2 strips, 5½" x 38½"
- 6 strips, 2½" x 42", for binding

From the red print, cut:
- 5 strips, 2" x 42"; crosscut into 96 squares, 2" x 2"

From the yellow star print, cut:
- 5 strips, 2" x 42"; crosscut into 96 squares, 2" x 2"
- 5 strips, 1½" x 42"

MAKING THE BLOCKS

You'll make 12 blocks for this quilt: 6 each in two different color arrangements. The secondary star design is created when the blocks are sewn together.

1. Sew a 2" x 6½" orange rectangle to the top and bottom of a 6½" duck print square as shown; press. Make six.

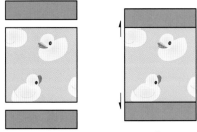

Make 6.

2. Sew a 2" red square to both ends of a 2" x 6½" teal rectangle as shown; press. Make 12. Sew these units to the remaining sides of each unit from step 1; press. Make six.

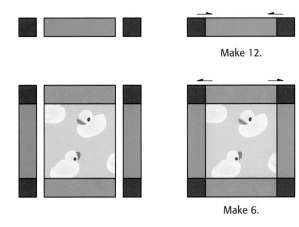

Make 12.

Make 6.

3. Repeat step 1 using the remaining 2" x 6½" teal rectangles and 6½" duck print squares. Make six.

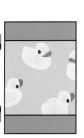

Make 6.

4. Sew a 2" red square to both ends of each remaining 2" x 6½" orange rectangle as shown; press. Sew these units to the remaining sides of each unit from step 3; press. Make six.

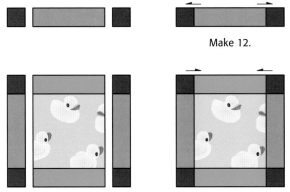

Make 12.

Make 6.

5. Referring to "Folded-Corner Piecing" on page 74 as needed, sew a 2" yellow square to both ends of each 2" x 9½" orange rectangle. Trim the excess fabric, leaving a ¼"-wide seam allowance; press. Repeat using the remaining 2" yellow squares and the 2" x 9½" teal rectangles. Make 24 of each.

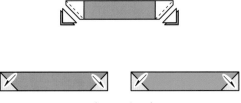

Make 24 of each.

6. Sew a yellow-and-teal unit from step 5 to the top and bottom of each unit from step 2; press. Make six.

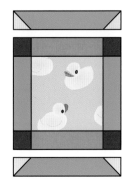
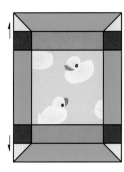

Make 6.

7. Repeat step 6 to sew a yellow-and-orange unit to the top and bottom of each unit from step 4. Make six.

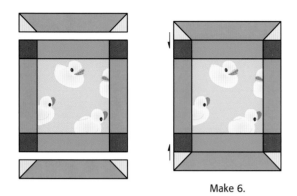

Make 6.

8. Sew a 2" red square to each remaining unit from step 5. Make 12 of each.

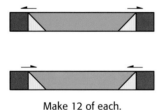

Make 12 of each.

9. Sew a yellow/orange/red unit from step 8 to the remaining sides of each unit from step 6; press. Sew a yellow/teal/red unit from step 8 to the remaining sides of each unit from step 7. Make six of each.

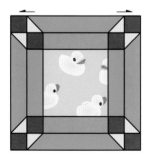 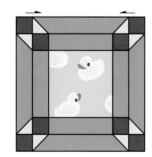

Make 6 of each.

ASSEMBLING THE QUILT

1. Refer to the assembly diagram below and arrange the blocks in four horizontal rows of three blocks each, alternating the two different blocks as shown. Sew the blocks into rows; press. Sew the rows together; press.

2. Sew the 1½" x 42" yellow strips together end to end to make one continuous strip. Refer to "Straight-Cut Borders" on pages 75–76 to measure, trim, and then sew a trimmed inner border to the sides, top, and bottom of the quilt. Press the seams toward the border.

3. Referring to the quilt photo on page 21, sew the 5½" x 38½" duck-print strips to the top and bottom of the quilt for the outer border, taking care to orient the ducks correctly. Press the seams toward the outer border. Sew the 5½" x 60½" strips to the sides; press.

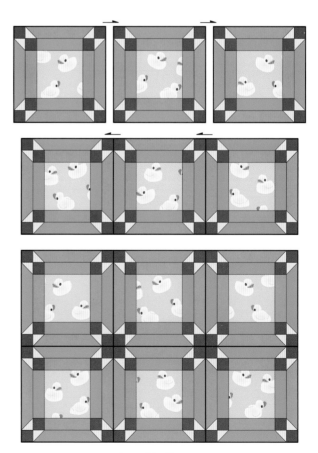

Assembly diagram

FINISHING THE QUILT

Refer to "Finishing" on pages 76–79 as needed to complete the following steps.

1. Layer the quilt top with the batting and backing. Baste the layers together.

2. Hand or machine quilt as desired. I didn't give Becky Marshall any direction for quilting this project, but it turned out just perfectly! She added feathers to the rubber duckies, creating a sense of whimsy—exactly what I was looking for!

3. Square up the quilt sandwich. Add a hanging sleeve if desired.

4. Using the 2½" x 42" duck print strips, make the binding and finish the edges of the quilt. Add a label if desired.

Quilt plan

"RUBBER DUCKIES" ALTERNATE

Asian prints are among my favorite novelty fabrics, but the motifs are generally on the large side. This block, with its wide-open center area, is perfect for showing off beautiful Asian prints, as you can see in this simple six-block table runner.

Pink Flamingos!

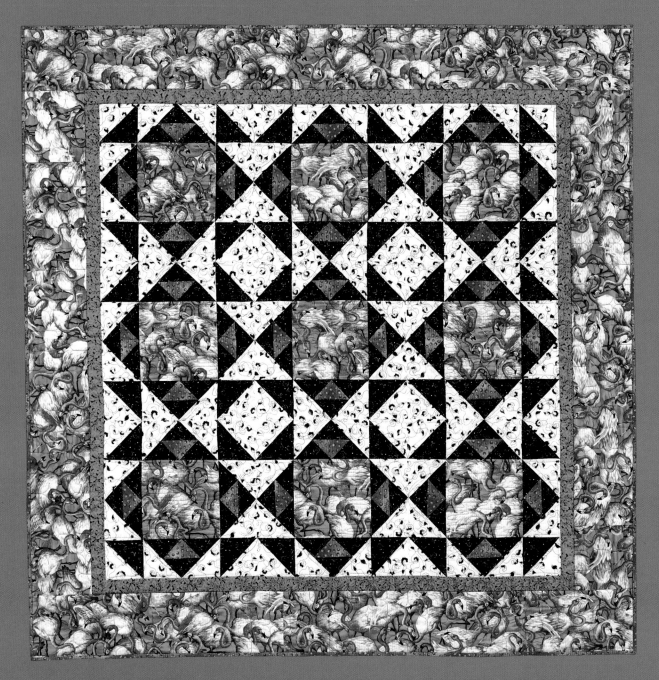

Made by Terry Martin, Snohomish, Washington. Quilted by Barb Dau. The theme song and opening to the old television show *Miami Vice* run through my head when I look at this quilt—not because of Don Johnson, but because of the scene with the pink flamingos running on the water and taking flight.

What is it with pink flamingos? They're everywhere! My best friend, Cornelia, received a plastic pink flamingo as a gift. You know—the kind that "flock" together as yard decoration. Well, this particular flamingo has a different outfit for every month so you can change his "clothes." Since she doesn't want it taken from the front yard, she keeps it inside, and her kids are just as eager as Cornelia to change that outfit every month. I personally can't wait for July to see the bird dressed in an Uncle Sam getup—right down to the beard and stovepipe hat!

This quilt in hot pinks, blacks, whites, and a punch of turquoise was a gas to make. Throw it over a white wicker chair and enjoy the summer's cool evening breeze.

Finished Quilt: 63" x 63"   **Finished Block:** 16" x 16"

MATERIALS

All yardages are based on 42"-wide fabric.

2⅞ yards of pink flamingo print for blocks, border, and binding

1¼ yards of white-with-black print for blocks

1¼ yards of black-with-white print for blocks

½ yard of teal tone-on-tone print for border

⅜ yard of pink tone-on-tone print for blocks

3⅞ yards of fabric for backing

69" x 69" piece of batting

CUTTING

All measurements include ¼"-wide seam allowances. Cut all strips across the width of the fabric (selvage to selvage).

From the pink tone-on-tone print, cut:

- 2 strips, 3¾" x 42"; crosscut into 18 squares, 3¾" x 3¾". Cut each square once diagonally to yield 2 half-square triangles (36 total).

From the black-with-white print, cut:

- 6 strips, 3¾" x 42"; crosscut into 54 squares, 3¾" x 3¾". Cut each square once diagonally to yield 2 half-square triangles (108 total).
- 3 strips, 4⅞" x 42"; crosscut into 18 squares, 4⅞" x 4⅞". Cut each square once diagonally to yield 2 half-square triangles (36 total).

From the white-with-black print, cut:

- 7 strips, 4⅞" x 42"; crosscut into 54 squares, 4⅞" x 4⅞". Cut each square once diagonally to yield 2 half-square triangles (108 total).

From the flamingo print, cut:

- 3 strips, 8½" x 42"; crosscut into 9 squares, 8½" x 8½"
- 7 strips, 6½" x 42"
- 7 strips, 2½" x 42", for binding

From the teal tone-on-tone print, cut:

- 6 strips, 2" x 42"

MAKING THE BLOCKS

You'll make nine blocks for this quilt.

1. Sew a pink half-square triangle and a small black-with-white half-square triangle together as shown; press. Make 36.

Make 36.

2. Sew the remaining small black-with-white half-square triangles to adjacent sides of each unit from step 1 as shown; press. Make 36.

Make 36.

3. Sew a white-with-black half-square triangle to the two short sides of each unit from step 2; press. Make 36.

Make 36.

4. Sew a unit from step 3 to opposite sides of each 8½" flamingo-print square; press. Make nine.

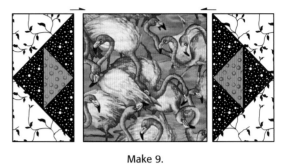

Make 9.

5. Sew a large black-with-white half-square triangle and a remaining white-with-black half-square triangle together as shown; press. Make 36.

Make 36.

6. Sew a unit from step 5 to opposite ends of each remaining unit from step 3 as shown; press. Make 18.

Make 18.

7. Sew a unit from step 6 to the top and bottom of each unit from step 4; press. Make nine.

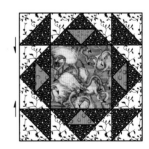

Make 9.

ASSEMBLING THE QUILT

1. Refer to the assembly diagram below and arrange the blocks in three horizontal rows of three blocks each, taking care with the orientation of the blocks if you have used a directional print. Sew the blocks into rows; press. Sew the rows together; press.

2. Sew the 2" x 42" teal strips together end to end to make one continuous strip. Refer to "Straight-Cut Borders" on pages 75–76 to measure, trim, and sew a trimmed inner border to the sides, top, and bottom of the quilt. Press the seams toward the border.

3. Repeat step 2 using the 6½" x 42" flamingo print outer-border strips.

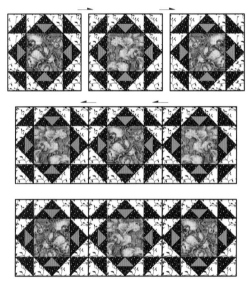

Assembly diagram

Continued on page 30

"PINK FLAMINGOS!" ALTERNATE

I used a group of novelty prints with a sewing theme to assemble this quick-and-easy, three-block table runner. It makes a perfect—and charming—covering for the small coffee table in my sewing room.

FINISHING THE QUILT

Refer to "Finishing" on pages 76–79 as needed to complete the following steps.

1. Layer the quilt top with the batting and backing. Baste the layers together.

2. Hand or machine quilt as desired. Barb Dau had fun quilting the flamingos with hot pink and black variegated threads. Given more open space in the blocks, she was able to use a number of designs, including a heart-shaped scroll, ripples of water, and a vertical "wallpaper" pattern.

3. Square up the quilt sandwich. Add a hanging sleeve if desired.

4. Using the 2½" x 42" flamingo print strips, make the binding and finish the edges of the quilt. Add a label if desired.

Quilt plan

Blueberry Buckle

Made by Terry Martin, Snohomish, Washington. Machine quilted by Barb Dau. When you take a close look, you'll discover that this is a very "polka-dotty" quilt. I was picking fabric for color and scale and realized afterward that the fabrics all have dots!

I've learned to really love blueberries. As a kid I thought they had an old, almost antique flavor to them. Now my daughter and I look forward to heading to our local blueberry farm, making freezer jam and cobbler, and freezing the rest for winter enjoyment. And my best friend makes the best Blueberry Buckle you've ever tasted!

Sometimes I get a little carried away with a theme, but who could find a quilt block called Blueberry Buckle and then resist the urge to seek just the right blueberry print fabric to make it work? I hope you find this a cheerful quilt, with its scheme of blue and yellow—a favorite color combination for quilters that has passed the test of time.

Finished Quilt: 54" x 54"   **Finished Block:** 10" x 10"

MATERIALS

All yardages are based on 42"-wide fabric.

2 yards of blueberry-and-yellow print for blocks, outer border, and binding

1 yard of dark blueberry print for blocks and middle border

⅞ yard of yellow print for blocks and inner border

¾ yard of green polka-dot print for blocks

3 yards of fabric for backing

60" x 60" piece of batting

CUTTING

All measurements include ¼"-wide seam allowances. Cut all strips across the width of the fabric (selvage to selvage).

From the green polka-dot print, cut:

- 4 strips, 2½" x 42"
- 6 strips, 1½" x 42"

From the blueberry-and-yellow print, cut:

- 5 strips, 1½" x 42"
- 2 strips, 4⅞" x 42"; crosscut into 16 squares, 4⅞" x 4⅞". Cut each square once diagonally to yield 2 half-square triangles (32 total).
- 6 strips, 4½" x 42"
- 6 strips, 2½" x 42", for binding

From the dark blueberry print, cut:

- 1 strip, 4½" x 42"
- 2 strips, 1½" x 42"
- 2 strips, 4⅞" x 42"; crosscut into 16 squares, 4⅞" x 4⅞". Cut each square once diagonally to yield 2 half-square triangles (32 total).
- 5 strips, 2¼" x 42"

From the yellow print, cut:

- 5 strips, 1½" x 42"
- 5 strips, 2⅞" x 42"; crosscut into 64 squares, 2⅞" x 2⅞". Cut each square once diagonally to yield 2 half-square triangles (128 total).
- 5 strips, 1¾" x 42"

MAKING THE BLOCKS

You'll make 16 Blueberry Buckle blocks for this quilt.

1. Arrange two 2½" x 42" green strips, two 1½" x 42" blueberry-and-yellow strips, and the 4½" x 42" dark blueberry strip as shown. Sew the strips together to make a strip set; press. Crosscut the strip set into 16 segments, 2½" wide.

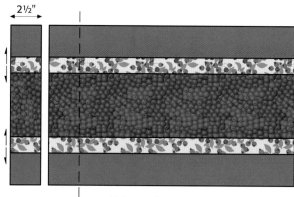

Make 1 strip set.
Cut 16 segments.

2. Arrange one 2½" x 42" green strip, one 1½" x 42" yellow strip, and one 1½" x 42" dark blueberry strip as shown. Sew the strips together to make a strip set; press. Make two. Crosscut the strip sets into 32 segments, 2½" wide.

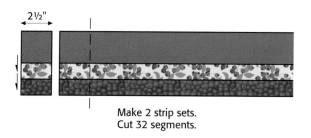

Make 2 strip sets.
Cut 32 segments.

3. Sew together one 1½" x 42" green strip and one 1½" x 42" yellow strip to make a strip set; press. Make three. Repeat using a 1½" x 42" green strip and a 1½" x 42" blueberry-and-yellow strip. Make three strip sets. Crosscut 64 segments, 1½" wide, from each set of strip sets (128 total).

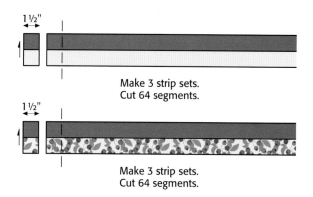

Make 3 strip sets.
Cut 64 segments.

Make 3 strip sets.
Cut 64 segments.

4. Sew one segment of each color combination from step 3 together to make a four-patch unit as shown; press. Make 64.

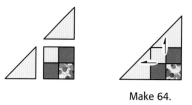

Make 64.

5. Sew a yellow half-square triangle to two adjacent sides of each four-patch unit from step 4 as shown; press. Make 64.

Make 64.

6. Sew a dark blueberry half-square triangle to the long edge of a unit from step 5 as shown; press. Make 32. Sew a blueberry-and-yellow half-square triangle to each remaining unit from step 5; press. Make 32.

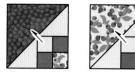

Make 32 of each.

7. Sew one of each unit from step 6 to opposite sides of each segment from step 2 as shown; press. Make 32.

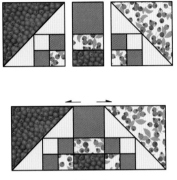

Make 32.

8. Sew each segment from step 1 between two units from step 7 as shown; press. Make 16.

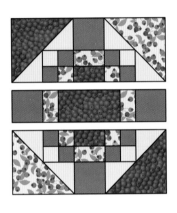

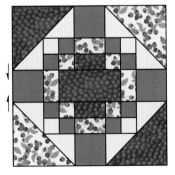

Make 16.

ASSEMBLING THE QUILT

1. Refer to the assembly diagram below and arrange the blocks in four horizontal rows of four blocks each as shown. Sew the blocks into rows; press. Sew the rows together; press.

2. Sew the 1¾" x 42" yellow strips together end to end to make one continuous strip. Refer to "Straight-Cut Borders" on pages 75–76 to measure, trim, and sew a trimmed inner border to the sides, top, and bottom of the quilt. Press the seams toward the border.

3. Repeat step 2 using the 2¼" x 42" dark blueberry strips to add the middle border and the 4½" x 42" blueberry-and-yellow strips to add the outer border to the sides, top, and bottom. Press the seams toward each newly added border.

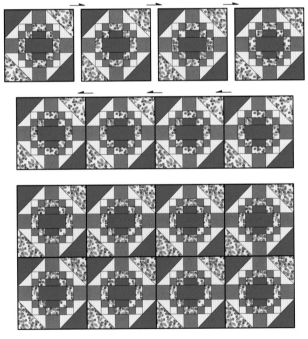

Assembly diagram

FINISHING THE QUILT

Refer to "Finishing" on pages 76–79 as needed to complete the following steps.

1. Layer the quilt top with the batting and backing. Baste the layers together.

2. Quilt as desired. Barb Dau created a wonderful allover pattern of swirls and feathers using a variegated thread. The borders were quilted with a ribbon design, and feathers were added in the outer border.

3. Square up the quilt sandwich. Add a hanging sleeve if desired.

4. Using the 2½" x 42" blueberry-and-yellow strips, make the binding and finish the edges of the quilt. Add a label if desired.

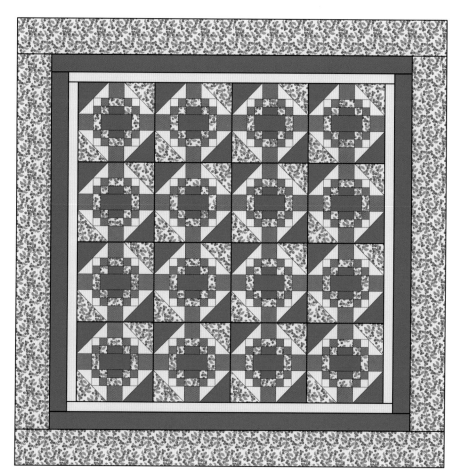

Quilt plan

The Red-and-Black Quilt

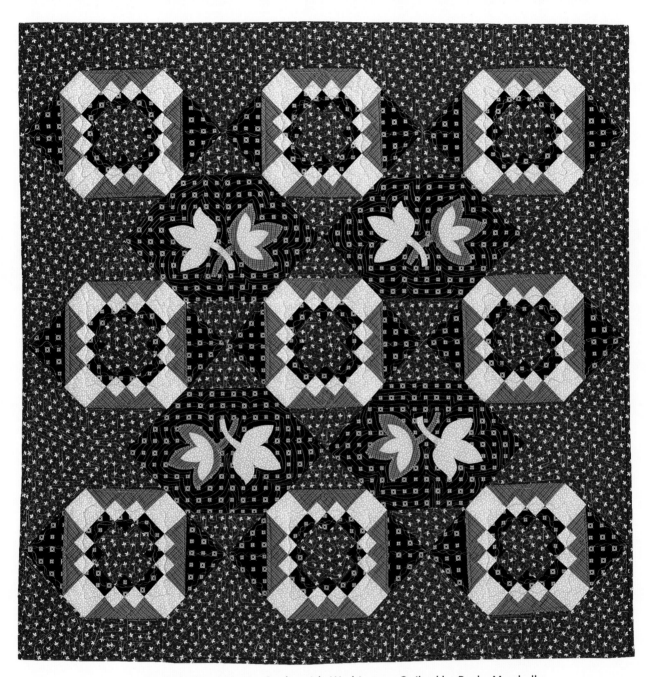

Made by Terry Martin, Snohomish, Washington. Quilted by Becky Marshall.
This quilt reminds me of that old riddle: what's black and white and read all over?

OK, you caught me! This quilt has nothing to do with novelty prints, but I'm using it as the partner to "Blueberry Buckle" anyway. Consider it a bonus project: I hope you enjoy making it!

When I was picking out the fabrics for this quilt, I wanted to get as far away from novelty prints as I could. One of my coworkers, Karen Soltys, is a talented craftswoman whose work I admire. She loves the homespun look and palette. The fabrics and colors in this quilt remind me of her style. Fabrics are always "talking" to me, telling me who would like these colors or that print, once again evoking memories of someone I know. My husband worries a little when I talk back to the fabric, but he's getting used to it.

Finished Quilt: 42½" x 42½"   **Finished Block:** 10" x 10"

MATERIALS

All yardages are based on 42"-wide fabric.

1⅞ yards of red print for blocks, side and corner setting triangles, and binding
1⅜ yards of black print for blocks
¾ yard of beige print for blocks and appliqués
⅝ yard of tan plaid for blocks and appliqués
2¾ yards of fabric for backing
49" x 49" piece of batting

CUTTING

All measurements include ¼"-wide seam allowances. Cut all strips across the width of the fabric (selvage to selvage).

From the beige print, cut:
- 4 strips, 2½" x 42"
- 4 strips, 1½" x 42"

From the black print, cut:
- 6 strips, 1½" x 42"
- 2 strips, 4⅞" x 42"; crosscut into 9 squares, 4⅞" x 4⅞". Cut each square once diagonally to yield 2 half-square triangles (18 total).
- 2 strips, 10½" x 42"; crosscut into 4 squares, 10½" x 10½"

From the red print, cut:

- 2 strips, 4½" x 42"; crosscut 1 strip into 8 squares, 4½" x 4½"
- 2 strips, 1½" x 42"
- 2 strips, 4⅞" x 42"; crosscut into 9 squares, 4⅞" x 4⅞". Cut each square once diagonally to yield 2 half-square triangles (18 total).
- 2 squares, 15½" x 15½"; cut each square twice diagonally to yield 4 quarter-square triangles (8 total).
- 2 squares, 8" x 8"; cut each square once diagonally to yield 2 half-square triangles (4 total).
- 5 strips, 2½" x 42", for binding

From the tan plaid, cut:

- 2 strips, 1½" x 42"
- 3 strips, 2⅞" x 42"; crosscut into 36 squares, 2⅞" x 2⅞". Cut each square once diagonally to yield 2 half-square triangles (72 total).

MAKING THE BLOCKS

You'll make a total of 13 blocks for this quilt: 9 Blueberry Buckle blocks and 4 appliqué leaf blocks.

1. Arrange two 2½" x 42" beige strips, two 1½" x 42" black strips, and one 4½" x 42" red strip as shown. Sew the strips together to make a strip set; press. Crosscut the strip set into nine segments, 2½" wide.

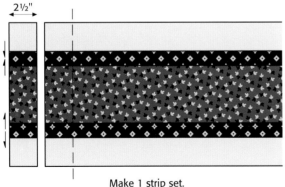

Make 1 strip set.
Cut 9 segments.

2. Arrange one 2½" x 42" beige strip, one 1½" x 42" black strip, and one 1½" x 42" red strip as shown. Sew the strips together to make a strip set; press. Make two. Crosscut the strip sets into 18 segments, 2½" wide.

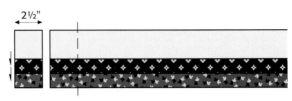

Make 2 strip sets.
Cut 18 segments.

3. Sew together one 1½" x 42" beige strip and one 1½" x 42" black strip to make a strip set; press. Make two strip sets. Repeat using 1½" x 42" beige strips and 1½" x 42" tan strips to make two strip sets. Crosscut 36 segments, 1½" wide, from each set of strip sets (72 total).

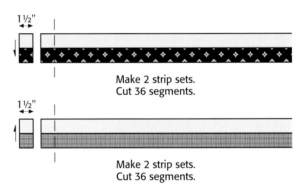

Make 2 strip sets.
Cut 36 segments.

Make 2 strip sets.
Cut 36 segments.

4. Sew one segment of each color combination from step 3 together to make a four-patch unit; press. Make 36.

Make 36.

5. Sew a tan half-square triangle to two adjacent sides of each four-patch unit from step 4 as shown; press. Make 36.

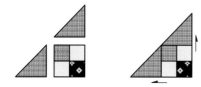

6. Sew a 4⅞" red half-square triangle to a unit from step 5 as shown; press. Make 18. Repeat to sew a black half-square triangle to each remaining unit from step 5; press. Make 18.

Make 18 of each.

7. Sew one of each unit from step 6 to opposite sides of each segment from step 2 as shown; press. Make 18.

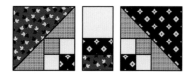

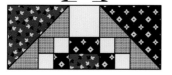

Make 18.

8. Sew each segment from step 1 between two units from step 7 as shown; press. Make nine.

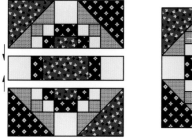

Make 9.

9. Referring to "Folded-Corner Piecing" on page 74 as needed, sew a 4½" red square to opposite corners of each 10½" black square as shown. Trim the excess fabric, leaving a ¼"-wide seam allowance; press. Make four.

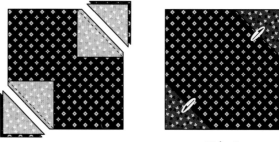

Make 4.

10. Use the patterns on page 41 to make templates for the leaf appliqués. Trace and cut out four large leaves (A) from the tan fabric and four medium leaves (B) and four small leaves (C) from the beige fabric. Refer to the photo on page 36 and the diagram below to position one of each appliqué shape on each block from step 9. Use your favorite appliqué method to appliqué the motifs in place. (I fused the appliqué to the block and machine stitched a buttonhole stitch around each of the motifs using beige thread.)

ASSEMBLING THE QUILT

Refer to the assembly diagram below and arrange the pieced blocks, the appliqué blocks, the red quarter-square side setting triangles, and the red half-square corner setting triangles in diagonal rows. Sew the blocks and side setting triangles into rows; press. Sew the rows together, adding the corner triangles last; press. Square up the quilt, making sure to maintain a ¼"-wide seam allowance around the edges.

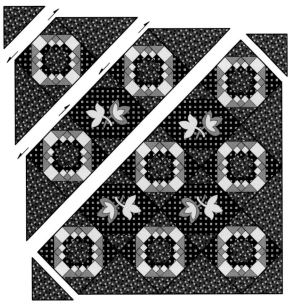

Assembly diagram

FINISHING THE QUILT

Refer to "Finishing" on pages 76–79 as needed to complete the following steps.

1. Layer the quilt top with the batting and backing. Baste the layers together.

2. Hand or machine quilt as desired. I asked Becky Marshall to use a simple echo stitch around the appliqués and have fun with the rest. She did a great job!

3. Square up the quilt sandwich. Add a hanging sleeve if desired.

4. Using the 2½" x 42" red strips, make the binding and finish the edges of the quilt. Add a label if desired.

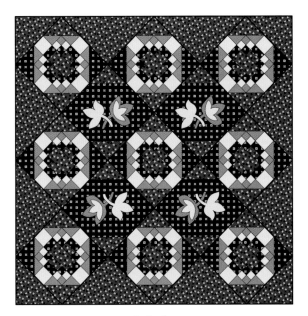

Quilt plan

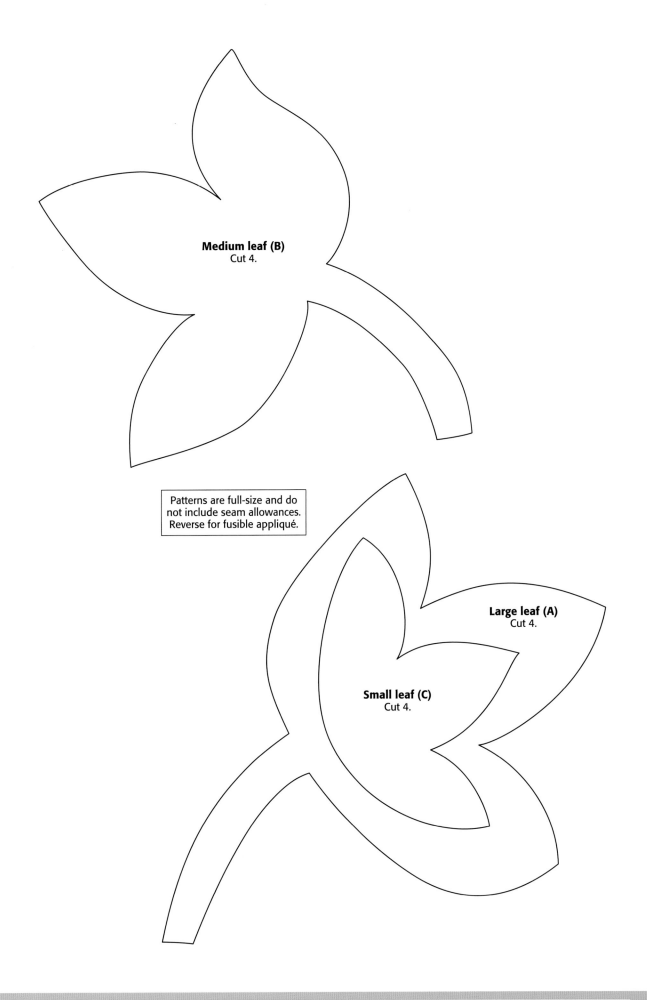

Medium leaf (B)
Cut 4.

Patterns are full-size and do
not include seam allowances.
Reverse for fusible appliqué.

Large leaf (A)
Cut 4.

Small leaf (C)
Cut 4.

Cherries Jubilee

Made by Terry Martin, Snohomish, Washington. Quilted by Becky Marshall. This quilt is a riot of cherries and lots of fun to use on the kitchen table. Protect the quilt with a piece of glass or heavy plastic.

To my mind, having a fabric stash that includes a variety of cherry prints is a must! I'm blessed to live in the Pacific Northwest, and I love the new crops of Bing and Rainier cherries that come from Yakima and Wenatchee, Washington, every year. This quilt, which I use as a tablecloth, explodes with cherries. It really jazzes up my kitchen table! Every meal seems just like a picnic. When you start with a large center panel, this quilt sews up quickly and is a perfect way to show off a theme print.

Becky Marshall quilted this project for me. When I first gave it to her, she stared at it silently. "Uh-oh," I said to myself. "She doesn't like it." When she came out of her daydream, she told me she was already thinking up designs and quilting it in her mind. Whew!!

Finished Quilt: 61" x 67"   **Finished Block:** 3" x 3" and 6" x 6"

MATERIALS

All yardages are based on 42"-wide fabric.

2 yards of black-background large-scale cherry print for quilt center and unpieced border 5

1⅛ yards of black-background medium-scale cherry print for blocks, unpieced border 3, and binding

⅞ yard of white-background cherry print with polka dots for blocks and unpieced border 4

⅔ yard of yellow-background cherry print for blocks

⅔ yard of red-and-yellow checkerboard print with cherries for blocks

⅜ yard of yellow checkerboard print with cherries for unpieced border 1

⅜ yard of black-background small-scale cherry print for unpieced border 2

⅜ yard of red checkerboard print with white cherries for blocks

3⅔ yards of fabric for backing (horizontal seam)

66" x 72" piece of batting

CUTTING

All measurements include ¼"-wide seam allowances. Cut all strips across the width of the fabric (selvage to selvage).

From the yellow checkerboard print with cherries, cut:

- 4 strips, 2½" x 42"; crosscut into:
  2 strips, 2½" x 24½"
  2 strips, 2½" x 21½"

From the black-background large-scale cherry print, cut:

- 1 rectangle, 18½" x 24½"
- 6 strips, 6½" x 42"

From the white-background cherry print with polka dots, cut:

- 5 strips, 2⅜" x 42"; crosscut into 72 squares, 2⅜" x 2⅜". Cut each square once diagonally to yield 2 half-square triangles (144 total).
- 6 strips, 2" x 42"

From the red checkerboard print with white cherries, cut:

- 3 strips, 2⅝" x 42"; crosscut into 36 squares, 2⅝" x 2⅝"

From the black-background small-scale cherry print, cut:

- 4 strips, 2" x 42"

From the black-background medium-scale cherry print, cut:

- 14 strips, 2½" x 42"

From the yellow-background cherry print, cut:

- 8 strips, 2½" x 42"

From the red-and-yellow checkerboard print with cherries, cut:

- 8 strips, 2½" x 42"

ASSEMBLING THE QUILT

This quilt top features a variety of simple borders, so it's easy to put together and really shows off the fun cherry prints. Two of the rows are pieced from blocks. You'll make 36 Square-in-a-Square blocks that are 3" x 3" and 26 Nine Patch blocks that are 6" x 6".

The section "Straight-Cut Borders" on pages 75–76 provides guidance for adding the borders; refer to the photo on page 42 and the quilt plan on page 46 for the proper placement of each row.

1. Sew the 2½" x 24½" yellow checkerboard strips to opposite sides of the 18½" x 24½" large-scale print rectangle. Press the seams toward the border. Sew the 2½" x 21½" strips to the top and bottom to complete unpieced border 1; press.

2. Sew a polka-dot half-square triangle to opposite sides of each 2⅝" red checkerboard square as shown; press. Sew polka-dot half-square triangles to the remaining sides; press. Make 36.

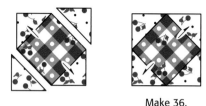

Make 36.

3. Sew nine blocks from step 2 together to make a row; press. Make four rows. Sew one row to opposite sides of the unit from step 1. Press the seams away from the pieced row. Sew the remaining rows to the top and bottom; press.

4. Sew the 2" x 42" black small-scale print strips together end to end to make one continuous strip. Refer to "Straight-Cut Borders" on pages 75–76 to measure, trim, and sew a trimmed unpieced border 2 to the sides, top, and bottom of the quilt. Press the seams toward the border.

5. Sew one 2½" x 42" yellow-background strip between two 2½" x 42" red-and-yellow checkerboard strips as shown to make a strip set; press. Make four strip sets. Crosscut the strip sets into 52 segments, 2½" wide.

2½"

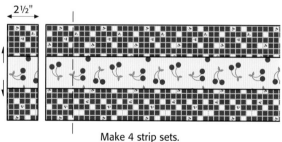

Make 4 strip sets.
Cut 52 segments.

continued on page 46

"Cherries Jubilee" Alternate

I love the changing seasons and am always ready for the next season to arrive. Just when I've had enough of summer, the cool breezes of Indian summer start to rustle the leaves from the trees and I'm anxious for autumn.

For this version, I modified "Cherries Jubilee" by making the center panel a square instead of a rectangle. The rich, dark, jewel-toned leaf fabrics will look great as a fall decoration in my home. Try using prints with a seasonal theme in your quilts, and you'll always welcome the next season—whether it's fall, winter, spring, or summer.

6. Sew one 2½" x 42" black medium-scale print strip between two 2½" x 42" yellow-background strips as shown to make a strip set; press. Make two strip sets. Crosscut the strip sets into 26 segments, 2½" wide.

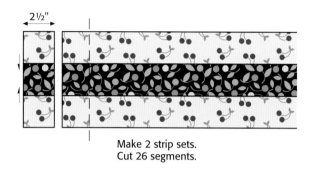

Make 2 strip sets.
Cut 26 segments.

7. Sew one segment from step 6 between two segments from step 5 as shown; press. Make 26.

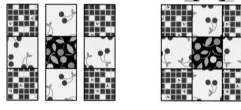

Make 26.

8. Sew six blocks from step 7 together to make a row; press. Make two rows. Sew the rows to opposite sides of the unit from step 4. Press the seams away from the pieced rows. Sew seven blocks from step 7 together to make a row; press. Make two rows and sew them to the top and bottom of the unit; press.

9. Repeat step 4 using five 2½" x 42" black medium-scale print strips, then the six 2" x 42" polka-dot strips, and finally the six 6½" x 42" black large-scale print strips to add unpieced borders 3, 4, and 5 to the unit from step 8. Press the seams toward each newly added border.

FINISHING THE QUILT

Refer to "Finishing" on pages 76–79 as needed to complete the following steps.

1. Layer the quilt top with the batting and backing. Baste the layers together.

2. Hand or machine quilt as desired. Becky Marshall knows how much I like cherries, so she stitched big and small cherries all over the quilt. I love it!

3. Square up the quilt sandwich. Add a hanging sleeve if desired.

4. Using the remaining 2½" x 42" black medium-scale print strips, make the binding and finish the edges of the quilt. Add a label if desired.

Quilt plan

Harvest

Made by Terry Martin, Snohomish, Washington. Machine quilted by Barb Dau. My husband looks forward as much as I do to changing the quilt on our bed each season. This is my first fall quilt.

W

While developing or designing a new project, I enjoy researching quilt blocks. I keep a file folder and inspiration book close by that I fill with interesting block designs, color combinations, settings, and so on. I came across this block and instantly knew what to do with it. It's called Squash Blossom and making it up in a harvest-themed print was a natural. I didn't have an autumn-themed quilt for my bed, and this large-scale block and the print I used are just right. I made pillowcases and a throw pillow to match. Don't you just love using up the leftovers?

Finished Quilt: 87" x 102"　　**Finished Block:** 15" x 15"

MATERIALS

All yardages are based on 42"-wide fabric.

- 4⅞ yards of harvest print for blocks and outer border
- 3 yards of gold tone-on-tone print for blocks
- 2 yards of dark corn print for checkerboard border and binding
- 1⅛ yards of light corn print for checker-board border
- ⅞ yard of burgundy print for blocks and inner border
- 7¾ yards of fabric for backing (horizontal seam)
- 93" x 108" piece of batting

CUTTING

All measurements include ¼"-wide seam allowances. Cut all strips across the width of the fabric (selvage to selvage).

From the burgundy print, cut:
- 2 strips, 6¼" x 42"; crosscut into 10 squares, 6¼" x 6¼". Cut each square twice diagonally to yield 4 quarter-square triangles (40 total).
- 7 strips, 2" x 42"

From the harvest print, cut:
- 2 strips, 6¼" x 42"; crosscut into 10 squares, 6¼" x 6¼". Cut each square twice diagonally to yield 4 quarter-square triangles (40 total).
- 8 strips, 3⅜" x 42"; crosscut into 80 squares, 3⅜" x 3⅜". Cut each square once diagonally to yield 2 half-square triangles (160 total).
- 4 strips, 5½" x 42"; crosscut into 40 rectangles, 3" x 5½"
- 4 strips, 10½" x 42"; crosscut into 40 rectangles, 3" x 10½"
- 10 strips, 6½" x 42"

From the gold tone-on-tone print, cut:
- 4 strips, 6¼" x 42"; crosscut into 20 squares, 6¼" x 6¼". Cut each square twice diagonally to yield 4 quarter-square triangles (80 total).
- 13 strips, 5½" x 42"; crosscut into 160 rectangles, 3" x 5½"

From the light corn print, cut:
- 10 strips, 3½" x 42"

From the dark corn print, cut:
- 10 strips, 3½" x 42"
- 10 strips, 2½" x 42", for binding

MAKING THE BLOCKS

You'll make 20 Squash Blossom blocks for this quilt.

1. Sew a burgundy quarter-square triangle and a harvest print quarter-square triangle together as shown; press. Make 40. Sew the units together in pairs as shown; press. Make 20.

Make 20.

2. Sew a harvest print half-square triangle to the two short sides of each gold quarter-square triangle as shown; press. Make 80.

Make 80.

3. Sew a 3" x 5½" harvest print rectangle to a unit from step 2 as shown; press. Make 40.

Make 40.

4. Sew a unit from step 1 between two units from step 3 as shown; press. Make 20.

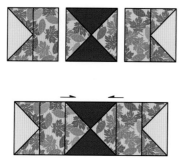

Make 20.

5. Sew a 3" x 5½" gold rectangle to each end of the remaining units from step 2; press. Make 40.

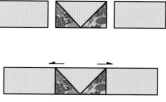

Make 40.

6. Referring to "Folded-Corner Piecing" on page 74 as needed, sew a remaining 3" x 5½" gold rectangle to opposite ends of a 3" x 10½" harvest print rectangle. Trim the excess fabric, leaving a ¼"-wide seam allowance; press. Make 40.

Make 40.

7. Sew a unit from step 5 to a unit from step 6 as shown; press. Make 40.

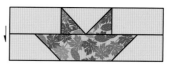

Make 40.

8. Sew a unit from step 4 between two units from step 7 as shown; press. Make 20.

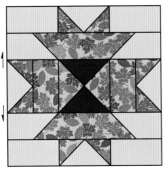

Make 20.

ASSEMBLING THE QUILT

Refer to the assembly diagram at right and arrange the blocks in five horizontal rows of four blocks each as shown. Sew the blocks into rows; press. Sew the rows together; press.

ADDING THE BORDERS

1. Sew the 2" x 42" burgundy strips together end to end to make one continuous strip. Refer to "Straight-Cut Borders" on pages 75–76 to measure, trim, and sew a trimmed inner border to the sides, top, and bottom of the quilt. Press the seams toward the border.

2. Sew together one 3½" x 42" light corn strip and one 3½" x 42" dark corn strip to make a

strip set; press. Make 10 strip sets. Crosscut the strip sets into 102 segments, 3½" wide.

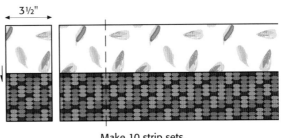

Make 10 strip sets.
Cut 102 segments.

3. Sew 26 segments from step 2 together to make a row; press. Make two rows. Sew the rows to opposite sides of the unit from step 1. Press the seams away from the pieced rows.

4. Sew 25 segments from step 2 together to make a row; press. Make two rows. Sew the rows to the top and bottom of the unit from step 3; press.

5. Repeat step 1 using the 6½" x 42" harvest print strips to add the outer border to the sides, top, and bottom of the quilt. Press the seams toward the newly added border.

Assembly diagram

FINISHING THE QUILT

Refer to "Finishing" on pages 76–79 as needed to complete the following steps.

1. Layer the quilt top with the batting and backing. Baste the layers together.

2. Hand or machine quilt as desired. Barb Dau created a wonderful lazy feather-and-swirl pattern across the surface of this large quilt.

3. Square up the quilt sandwich. Add a hanging sleeve if desired.

4. Using the 2½" x 42" dark corn strips, make the binding and finish the edges of the quilt. Add a label if desired.

Quilt plan

"HARVEST" ALTERNATE

It amazes me how choice of fabric, color, and value placement can completely change the character of a quilt block. The blocks in this simple table runner, with its cool colors and fabric that mimics stained glass, look nothing like the warm-toned blocks in "Harvest." This table runner is easy to assemble since it includes only three blocks and two simple framing borders. It truly makes up in just an afternoon. I love taking advantage of large quilt blocks to make something quick and easy with big impact.

Garden Party

Made by Terry Martin, Snohomish, Washington. Quilted by Becky Marshall. It's picnic time! Grab the picnic basket, pink lemonade on ice, and this adorable quilt for a fun day with your family in the backyard or at your favorite lake.

Although I don't necessarily count floral prints as novelty or theme fabric, this pretty floral had a china-plate border print along both selvages, so I stretched my usual definition to include it. I love this print and couldn't wait to use it. It is in my nature to use every bit of fabric, so even though the border portion wasn't my favorite, I decided to incorporate it into the quilt. Voilá—instant border! With some extra planning I could have used the border print in the block, but that would have required extra math—need I say more?

I've listed the border fabric separately in the materials list. If you use a fabric that already has a border print on one or both edges, you'll need to calculate extra yardage for the blocks and binding to compensate for the border width.

Finished Quilt: 60" x 72¾" ~ **Finished Block:** 9" x 9"

MATERIALS

All yardages are based on 42"-wide fabric.

3⅛ yards of floral print for blocks, setting triangles, and binding
1 yard of dish print for border
¾ yard of blue print for blocks
¾ yard of brown print for blocks
3⅓ yards of fabric for backing (horizontal seam)
66" x 79" piece of batting

CUTTING

All measurements include ¼"-wide seam allowances. Cut all strips across the width of the fabric (selvage to selvage).

From the brown print, cut:
- 4 strips, 2" x 42"
- 4 strips, 3½" x 42"

From the floral print, cut:
- 8 strips, 2" x 42"
- 4 strips, 3½" x 42"
- 3 strips, 9½" x 42"; crosscut into 12 squares, 9½" x 9½"
- 2 strips, 14" x 42"; crosscut into 4 squares, 14" x 14". Cut each square twice diagonally to yield 4 quarter-square triangles (16 total). You'll have 2 triangles left over.
- 2 squares, 7¼" x 7¼"; cut each square once diagonally to yield 2 half-square triangles (4 total)
- 7 strips, 2½" x 42", for binding

From the blue print, cut:
- 4 strips, 2" x 42"
- 4 strips, 3½" x 42"

From the dish print, cut:
- 7 strips, 5" x 42"

Making the Blocks

1. Arrange two 2" x 42" floral strips, one 3½" x 42" floral strip, and two 2" x 42" brown strips as shown. Sew the strips together to make a strip set; press. Make two strip sets. Crosscut the strip sets into 20 segments, 3½" wide.

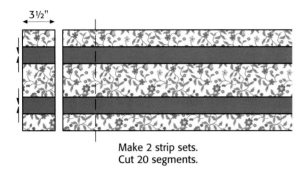

Make 2 strip sets.
Cut 20 segments.

2. Arrange two 2" x 42" blue strips, two 2" x 42" floral strips, and one 3½" x 42" brown strip as shown. Sew the strips together to make a strip set; press. Make two strip sets. Crosscut the strip sets into 40 segments, 2" wide.

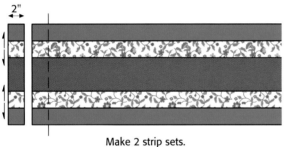

Make 2 strip sets.
Cut 40 segments.

3. Arrange two 3½" x 42" blue strips and one 3½" x 42" floral strip as shown. Sew the strips together to make a strip set; press. Make two strip sets. Crosscut the strip sets into 40 segments, 2" wide.

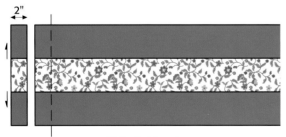

Make 2 strip sets.
Cut 40 segments.

4. Arrange and sew two segments each from steps 2 and 3 and one segment from step 1 as shown; press. Make 20.

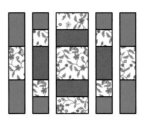
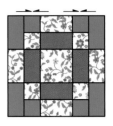

Make 20.

Assembling the Quilt

Refer to the assembly diagram below and arrange the blocks, 9½" floral squares, floral quarter-square side setting triangles, and floral half-square corner setting triangles in diagonal rows. Sew the blocks, squares, and side setting triangles into rows; press. Sew the rows together, adding the corner triangles last; press. Square up the quilt, making sure to maintain a ¼"-wide seam allowance around the edges.

Assembly diagram

ADDING THE BORDERS

Sew the 5" x 42" dish print strips together end to end to make one continuous strip. Refer to "Straight-Cut Borders" on pages 75–76 to measure, trim, and sew a trimmed border to the sides, top, and bottom of the quilt. Press the seams toward the border.

FINISHING THE QUILT

Refer to "Finishing" on pages 76–79 as needed to complete the following steps.

1. Layer the quilt top with the batting and backing. Baste the layers together.

2. Hand or machine quilt as desired. Becky Marshall used a light blue thread to create a lacy featherstitch in the blocks and soft stippling in the open spaces. She added a grid pattern over the dishes in the border to keep them from falling off!

3. Square up the quilt sandwich. Add a hanging sleeve if desired.

4. Using the 2½" x 42" floral strips, make the binding and finish the edges of the quilt. Add a label if desired.

Quilt plan

"GARDEN PARTY" ALTERNATE

I don't know of any other vegetable or gourd that enjoys quite the fame of the Halloween pumpkin. It has been a time-honored tradition in my family to pick out pumpkins to carve for Halloween. I remember my father insisted on cutting the top out for us, but we were responsible for removing all the "guts" and designing the face. One year my dad carved out ears for his pumpkin and we kids thought it was a pretty radical thing to do because we were such staunch traditionalists. So many wonderful memories: old candle stubs, the smell of pumpkin as the lit candle singed its lid, kids dressing up in old sheets to go trick-or-treating up and down the neighborhood—and the haul of candy wasn't bad either!

Now my daughter and I run for the door when the doorbell rings on Halloween. We can't wait to see what little ghouls and goblins lie in wait, and to greet their parents on the sidewalk, holding up coffee mugs in salute.

Trick or treat, and Happy Halloween!

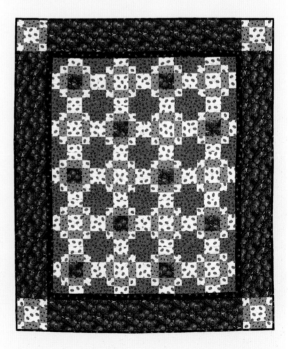

Made by Terry Martin, Snohomish, Washington. Quilted by Barb Dau. Mossy green colors are fun to work with but can be a bit tricky to coordinate. They tend to assume a chameleon-like quality, changing shade when you try to match them with other fabrics.

Eastern Washington has some of the most beautiful fruit orchards I've ever seen. My family and I vacation in the Wenatchee area a couple of times a year, usually in August or September during harvest. We can't wait to hit the local fruit stands for fresh fruit, preserves, and pressed juices. The peaches are the size of softballs, the apples are crisp, and the pears are so juicy you need two napkins, a shirt you don't mind messing up, and a trip to the restroom to wash afterwards! We load up the car for the drive back over the mountains to Western Washington, smelling the sweet fragrance of our delicious fruit all the way home.

This pear fabric really caught my eye! I collect all sorts of fruit, veggie, and kitschy kitchen fabric, but this print had an aura of sophistication. I picked rich colors all within a mossy green palette for a traditional, stately look. I plan to hang this quilt in our formal dining room.

Be sure to take a look at the alternate version on page 61. It's so eye-opening and fun to create the same pattern in different fabrics. The two quilts are basically the same but—surprisingly—also totally different!

Finished Quilt: 53" x 53"   **Finished Block:** 12" x 12"

MATERIALS

All yardages are based on 42"-wide fabric.

1¾ yards of medium green print for blocks and setting triangles

1½ yards of dark green print for blocks and setting triangles

1⅜ yards of pear print for blocks and binding

⅞ yard of light green print for blocks

3⅓ yards of fabric for backing

57" x 57" piece of batting

CUTTING

All measurements include ¼"-wide seam allowances. Cut all strips across the width of the fabric (selvage to selvage).

From the dark green print, cut:
- 14 strips, 2½" x 42"; crosscut 10 strips into:
  36 squares, 2½" x 2½"
  20 rectangles, 2½" x 12½"
- 2 strips, 4½" x 42"

From the pear print, cut:
- 2 strips, 4½" x 42"
- 10 strips, 2½" x 42"
- 1 strip, 6½" x 42"; crosscut into 4 squares, 6½" x 6½"

From the medium green print, cut:
- 6 strips, 2⅞" x 42"; crosscut into 72 squares, 2⅞" x 2⅞". Cut each square once diagonally to yield 2 half-square triangles (144 total).
- 6 strips, 2½" x 42"; crosscut into:
  8 rectangles, 2½" x 8½"
  8 rectangles, 2½" x 12½"
  8 squares, 2½" x 2½"
- 2 squares, 14¼" x 14¼"; cut each square twice diagonally to yield 4 quarter-square triangles (8 total).
- 2 squares, 7⅜" x 7⅜"; cut each square once diagonally to yield 2 half-square triangles (4 total).

From the light green print, cut:
- 2 strips, 5¼" x 42"; crosscut into 9 squares, 5¼" x 5¼". Cut each square twice diagonally to yield 4 quarter-square triangles (36 total).
- 3 strips, 2⅞" x 42"; crosscut into 36 squares, 2⅞" x 2⅞". Cut each square once diagonally to yield 2 half-square triangles (72 total).
- 4 strips, 1½" x 42"; crosscut into:
  8 rectangles, 1½" x 6½"
  8 rectangles, 1½" x 8½"

MAKING THE BLOCKS

You'll make 13 blocks for this quilt: 9 of block A and 4 of block B.

BLOCK A

1. Arrange two 2½" x 42" dark green strips and one 4½" x 42" pear-print strip as shown. Sew the strips together to make a strip set; press. Make two strip sets. Crosscut the strip sets into nine segments, 4½" wide.

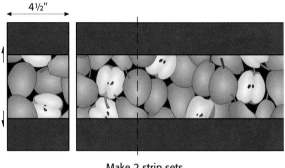

Make 2 strip sets.
Cut 9 segments.

2. Arrange two 2½" x 42" pear-print strips and one 4½" x 42" dark green strip as shown. Sew the strips together to make a strip set; press. Make two strip sets. Crosscut the strip sets into 18 segments, 2½" wide.

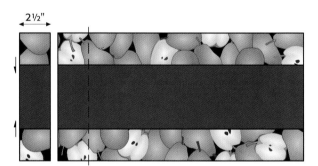

Make 2 strip sets.
Cut 18 segments.

3. Sew one segment from step 1 between two segments from step 2 as shown; press. Make nine.

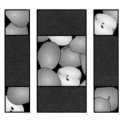 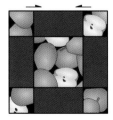

Make 9.

4. Sew a 2⅞" medium green half-square triangle to the two short sides of each light green quarter-square triangle as shown; press. Make 36.

Make 36.

5. Sew the remaining 2⅞" medium green half-square triangles and the light green half-square triangles together as shown; press. Make 72.

Make 72.

6. Sew a unit from step 4 between two units from step 5 as shown; press. Make 36.

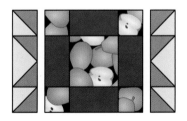

Make 36.

7. Sew each unit from step 3 between two units from step 6 as shown; press. Make nine.

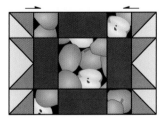

Make 9.

8. Sew a 2½" dark green square to each end of the remaining units from step 6; press. Make 18.

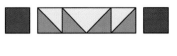

Make 18.

9. Sew one unit from step 7 between two units from step 8 as shown; press. Make nine.

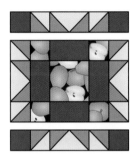

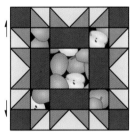

Make 9.

BLOCK B

1. Sew a 1½" x 6½" light green rectangle to opposite sides of each 6½" pear print square as shown; press. Sew a 1½" x 8½" light green rectangle to the top and bottom; press. Make four.

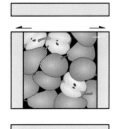

Make 4.

2. Sew a 2½" x 8½" medium green rectangle to opposite sides of each unit from step 1 as shown; press. Sew a 2½" x 12½" medium green rectangle to the top and bottom; press. Make four.

Make 4.

ASSEMBLING THE QUILT

1. Sew a 2½" x 12½" dark green rectangle to one short side of each medium green quarter-square side setting triangle as shown; press. Make eight.

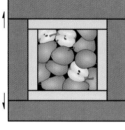

Make 8.

2. Sew a 2½" medium green square to the end of one 2½" x 12½" dark green rectangle as shown; press. Make eight.

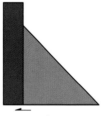

Make 8.

3. Sew each unit from step 2 to the remaining short side of each triangle unit from step 1 as shown; press. Trim the excess green strips even with the diagonal edge of the triangle. Make eight.

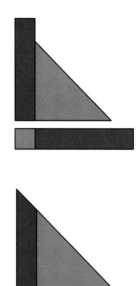

Make 8.

4. Center and sew a remaining 2½" x 12½" dark green rectangle to the long edge of each medium green half-square corner setting triangle as shown; press and trim. Make four.

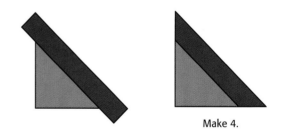

Make 4.

5. Refer to the assembly diagram on page 61 and arrange the A and B blocks, the quarter-square side setting triangles from step 3, and the half-square corner setting triangles from step 4 in diagonal rows. Sew the blocks and side setting triangles into rows; press. Sew the rows together, adding the corner triangles last; press. Square up the quilt to 53½" x 53½".

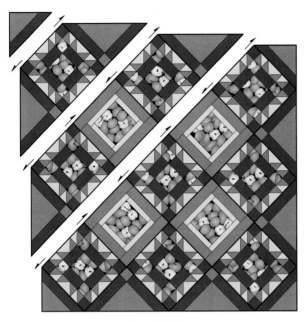

Assembly diagram

FINISHING THE QUILT

Refer to "Finishing" on pages 76–79 as needed to complete the following steps.

1. Layer the quilt top with the batting and backing. Baste the layers together.

2. Hand or machine quilt as desired. Barb Dau really outdid herself on this quilt. Each fabric is quilted with a different design, and the open spaces are quilted with beautiful feathers.

3. Square up the quilt sandwich. Add a hanging sleeve if desired.

4. Using the remaining 2½" x 42" pear print strips, make the binding and finish the edges of the quilt. Add a label if desired.

"PEARS" ALTERNATE

From sophisticated pears to whimsical celestial fabric—don't you just love novelty prints? I discovered this fabric while shopping with my daughter, McKenzie, and my best friend, Cornelia. Cornelia has a passion for celestial themes and after she took what she wanted off the bolt, I snagged the rest. I usually buy fabric to add to my stash but this one went right home, to the cutting table, and into a quilt within three days. When the inspiration hits, go for it!

Christmas Wreath

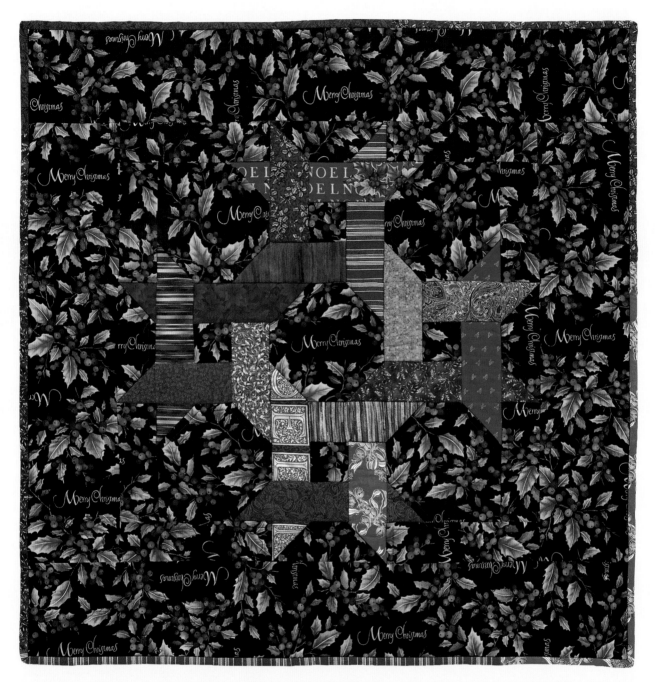

Made and quilted by Terry Martin, Snohomish, Washington. The next time I make this quilt, it will be in pretty floral fabrics to welcome spring and summer!

One main fabric and scraps or fat eighths of supporting prints make this quilt a super quick-and-easy project. At first I was worried about the "Merry Christmas" script that appeared on the key fabric. How was I going to make sure all the words would face in a readable direction? Then I discovered that the words were facing every which way on the fabric, so I didn't need to worry any more. What a relief! Lesson learned: no matter how hard you try to have all the fabrics face the "right way" on your quilt, sometimes it's impossible, so just let it go and have fun.

Speaking of having fun: what do you think of the fabrics I used for the alternate version of this quilt on page 66? The main fabric really is a Christmas print—believe it or not—but with a wonderful tropical twist.

Finished Quilt: 39½" x 39½"   **Finished Block:** 7½" x 7½"

MATERIALS

All yardages are based on 42"-wide fabric unless otherwise noted. Fat eighths measure 9" x 21".

1¾ yards of black "Merry Christmas" print for blocks and border

Scraps or fat eighths of 4 green prints and 12 red prints for blocks

½ yard of fabric for binding*

2½ yards of fabric for backing**

44" x 44" piece of batting

* I had enough scraps in the red prints to piece a scrappy binding.
** If your fabric measures a full 44" wide after it has been laundered, you'll need only 1¼ yards of backing fabric.

CUTTING

All measurements include ¼"-wide seam allowances. Cut all strips across the width of the fabric (selvage to selvage).

From *each* of the 16 scraps or fat eighths of green and red prints, cut:
- 1 rectangle, 3" x 5½"
- 1 square, 3" x 3"

NOTE: You'll need to cut more squares later in the project; fabrics will be determined by the layout of the quilt center.

From the black "Merry Christmas" print, cut:
- 4 strips, 3" x 42"; crosscut into:
  4 squares, 3" x 3"
  8 rectangles, 3" x 8"
  4 rectangles, 3" x 10½"
- 5 squares, 8" x 8"
- 4 strips, 6½" x 42"

From the binding fabric, cut:
- 5 strips, 2½" x 42"

MAKING THE BLOCKS

1. Sew a 3" x 5½" green rectangle to the bottom of each 3" Christmas print square, stitching only halfway across the edge as shown; press. Make four.

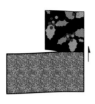

Make 4.

2. Sew a 3" x 5½" red rectangle to the right edge of each unit from step 1 as shown; press. Make four.

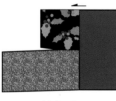

Make 4.

3. Sew a 3" x 5½" red rectangle to the top edge of each unit from step 2 as shown; press. Sew a third 3" x 5½" red rectangle to the left side of each unit; press. Make four. Complete the partial seam stitched in step 1; press.

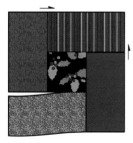 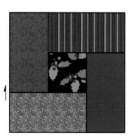

Make 4.

4. Refer to the photo on page 62 and the diagram at upper right. Arrange the blocks from step 3 and the 8" Christmas print squares in three horizontal rows of three blocks each, alternating them as shown. Rearrange the blocks until you're satisfied with the look.

(I chose to place the four green prints in the center.)

Once you have settled on an arrangement, fold the 3" red and green squares on the diagonal and place them on the corners of each 8" Christmas square so they match the red or green print in the block beside it; pin.

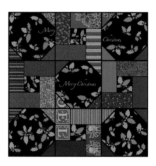

5. Refer to "Folded-Corner Piecing" on page 74. Working one block at a time, sew the appropriate 3" red or green squares to the designated corners of each 8" Christmas print block. Trim the excess fabric, leaving a ¼"-wide seam allowance; press. Make five, returning each block to the layout as the block is completed.

 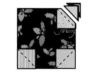

6. Sew the blocks into rows. Press the seams in opposite directions from row to row. Sew the rows together; press.

7. Return the quilt center to your design surface. Center the 3" x 8" Christmas print rectangles on the top, bottom, and side edges of the quilt as shown.

8. As you did in step 4, fold, place, and pin 3" red and green squares on the 3" x 8" Christmas print rectangles, matching the fabrics in the adjacent blocks. (Here's where you'll need to cut extra 3" red and green squares.) Working one unit at a time, use the folded-corner piecing method to sew the squares to the ends of the 3" x 8" Christmas print rectangles as shown; press. Make four, returning each unit to the layout as the unit is completed.

Make 4.

9. Fill in the top and bottom rows of the quilt with the remaining 3" x 8" Christmas print rectangles, and the side rows with the 3" x 10½" Christmas print rectangles as shown. Sew together three 3" x 8" rectangles (one pieced and two unpieced) to make a border. Press the seams away from the center (pieced) rectangle. Make two and sew to the top and bottom of the quilt. Press the seams toward the newly added border.

10. Repeat step 9 using the 3" x 8" pieced rectangles and the 3" x 10½" unpieced rectangles and sew to the sides of the quilt; press.

11. Sew the 6½" x 42" Christmas print strips together end to end to make one continuous strip. Refer to "Straight-Cut Borders" on pages 75–76 to measure, trim, and sew a trimmed border to the sides, top, and bottom of the quilt. Press the seams toward the border.

FINISHING THE QUILT

Refer to "Finishing" on pages 76–79 as needed to complete the following steps.

1. Layer the quilt top with the batting and backing. Baste the layers together.

2. Hand or machine quilt as desired. I machine quilted in the ditch around the wreath with matching green and red thread. I used black thread to stitch around the holly leaves and berries and around the "Merry Christmas" script to highlight each motif.

3. Square up the quilt sandwich. Add a hanging sleeve if desired.

4. Using the 2½" x 42" strips, make the binding and finish the edges of the quilt. Add a label if desired.

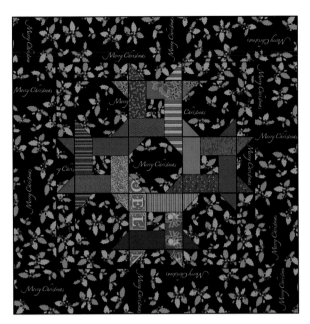

Quilt plan

"CHRISTMAS WREATH" ALTERNATE

Believe it or not, the main fabric in this quilt is also a Christmas print—but with a definite twist! The citrus colors add a lot of punch to this little quilt and it was a lot of fun picking out the wreath fabrics. Not your typical holiday quilt, is it? Make up this wreath using any seasonal theme print and use it for a door quilt. I think it would be great in patriotic prints for the Fourth of July.

Be My Valentine

Made and quilted by Terry Martin, Snohomish, Washington. This quilt reminds me of elementary school when we made valentines by hand and stuffed them in everyone's decorated shoe box. I couldn't wait to see who wanted to "Be Mine!" It was never a boy.

All things vintage appeal to me, and this little antique valentine print is pretty darn cute. A simple Snowball block really lets this novelty print shine. The alternate block adds movement and framing to the quilt. Just a reminder: if you use a directional print, be careful about the orientation of the design when you sew the rows of blocks together.

Finished Quilt: 48" x 48" ⟳ **Finished Block:** 8" x 8"

MATERIALS

All yardages are based on 42"-wide fabric.

1⅜ yards of blue print for blocks, pieced border, and binding

1 yard of red heart print for blocks and border corner squares

⅞ yard of vintage valentine print for blocks

⅞ yard of white-background floral print for blocks and pieced border

⅜ yard of yellow print for blocks and border corner squares

3 yards of fabric for backing

52" x 52" piece of batting

5 yards of medium-width yellow rickrack

CUTTING

All measurements include ¼"-wide seam allowances. Cut all strips across the width of the fabric (selvage to selvage).

From the red heart print, cut:

- 4 strips, 2½" x 42"; crosscut into 48 squares, 2½" x 2½"
- 3 strips, 2⅞" x 42"; crosscut into 34 squares, 2⅞" x 2⅞". Cut each square once diagonally to yield 2 half-square triangles (68 total).
- 3 strips, 3⅜" x 42"; crosscut into 52 rectangles, 1⅞" x 3⅜

From the vintage valentine print, cut:

- 3 strips, 8½" x 42"; crosscut into 12 squares, 8½" x 8½"

From the blue print, cut:

- 2 strips, 2⅞" x 42"; crosscut into 26 squares, 2⅞" x 2⅞". Cut each square once diagonally to yield 2 half-square triangles (52 total).
- 4 strips, 2⅜" x 42"; crosscut into 52 squares, 2⅜" x 2⅜". Cut each square once diagonally to yield 2 half-square triangles (104 total).
- 10 strips, 2½" x 42"

From the white-background floral print, cut:

- 2 strips, 5¼" x 42"; crosscut into 13 squares, 5¼" x 5¼". Cut each square twice diagonally to yield 4 quarter-square triangles (52 total).
- 5 strips, 2½" x 42"

From the yellow print, cut:

- 2 strips, 3⅜" x 42"; crosscut into 17 squares, 3⅜" x 3⅜"

MAKING THE BLOCKS

You'll make a total of 25 blocks for this quilt: 12 of block A and 13 of block B.

Block A

Referring to "Folded-Corner Piecing" on page 74 as needed, sew a 2½" red square to each corner of an 8½" valentine-print square as shown. Trim the excess fabric, leaving a ¼"-wide seam allowance; press. Make 12.

Make 12.

Block B

1. Sew a red half-square triangle and a blue large half-square triangle together as shown; press. Make 52.

Make 52.

2. Sew a blue small half-square triangle to adjacent sides of each unit from step 1 as shown; press. Make 52.

Make 52.

3. Sew a 1⅞" x 3⅜" red rectangle to each unit from step 2; press. Make 52.

Make 52.

4. Sew a floral quarter-square triangle to two adjacent sides of 26 units from step 3 as shown; press.

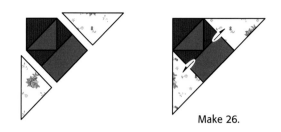

Make 26.

5. Sew a 3⅜" yellow square between two remaining units from step 3; press. Make 13.

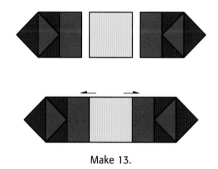

Make 13.

6. Sew each unit from step 5 between two units from step 4; press. Make 13.

Make 13.

ASSEMBLING THE QUILT

Refer to the assembly diagram below and arrange the blocks in five horizontal rows of five blocks each, alternating the A and B blocks as shown. Sew the blocks into rows; press. Sew the rows together; press.

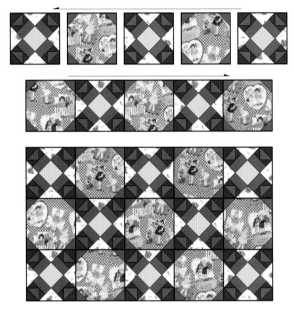

Assembly diagram

ADDING THE BORDERS

1. Sew together one 2½" x 42" blue strip and one 2½" x 42" floral strip to make a strip set; press. Make five strip sets. Crosscut the strip sets into 80 segments, 2½" wide.

2½"

Make 5 strip sets.
Cut 80 segments.

2. Sew 20 segments from step 1 together to make a row as shown; press. Make four rows. Sew two of the rows to opposite sides of the quilt. Press the seams toward the checkerboard borders.

Make 4.

3. Sew two red half-square triangles to opposite sides of each remaining 3⅜" yellow square as shown; press. Sew red triangles to the remaining sides; press. Make four.

Make 4.

4. Sew a unit from step 3 to each end of the remaining rows from step 2; press. Make two. Sew to the top and bottom of the quilt; press.

Quilt plan

Finishing the Quilt

Refer to "Finishing" on pages 76–79 as needed to complete the following steps.

1. Layer the quilt top with the batting and backing. Baste the layers together.

2. Hand or machine quilt as desired. This quilt has a lot going on, so I simply stitched in the ditch, allowing the fabrics to really show their stuff.

3. Square up the quilt sandwich. Add a hanging sleeve if desired.

4. Using the remaining 2½" x 42" blue strips, make the binding and finish the edges of the quilt. Add a label if desired.

5. Topstitch the yellow rickrack over the seam between the quilt center and the checkerboard border.

"Be My Valentine" Alternate

I thought you might enjoy seeing a soft, or blended, floral wall hanging—a real change from the primary colors of the valentine quilt. This floral quilt lends itself to a pretty, romantic decor.

Quiltmaking Basics

This section describes all the necessary elements for successfully completing your project, from choosing fabric and assembling essential tools for quiltmaking, to chain piecing, pressing, adding borders, making a quilt sandwich, quilting, binding, and finally, adding a hanging sleeve and label.

FABRIC, GLORIOUS FABRIC!

I'm not much of a mall shopper, but give me a couple of hours to kill in a fabric store or quilt shop and I'm in seventh heaven. I'm amazed by the fabrics being produced these days: the colors, textures, and designs are truly inspiring. I feel privileged to be quilting at a time when I can browse through dozens of racks of bolts of cotton fabric.

For quilting, I use 100%-cotton fabric. I find that cotton presses well and keeps its shape during the piecing process.

Try to buy the best-quality cotton fabric you can afford. Support your local quilt shop and fabric stores by buying your fabric and supplies there. Share your love of fabric with a young person. Teach her or him to quilt so that these shops can continue to support this wonderful fiber art form for a long time. And now I will step off my soapbox!

Yardage requirements are provided for all projects in this book and are based on fabric that is 42" wide when it comes off the bolt.

To prewash or not to prewash? That is the question, and it's one that sparks constant debate among quilters. I don't prewash fabric except to control shrinkage when I'm using muslin or flannel. I also wash batiks, but only

SHOPPING TIP

I'm always surprised when I show my quilts and the audience wants to see the back as well as the front. They usually want to see the machine quilting, but they always comment on the fabric. "How can you use such beautiful fabric for the back of a quilt?" they wonder.

Whenever possible, I try to match the fabric on the back of the quilt to the theme or color on the front. I have the luxury of using great fabric on the back of my quilts because I'm diligent about shopping the fabric sale rack. The fabrics I find there are usually nice-quality cotton goods that just—for whatever reason—didn't sell. I buy 5 to 10 yards off a bolt just to be used for backings. This way I always have sufficient fabric on hand, usually at a fraction of the original price.

when I'm using them in a lap or larger-sized quilt, not for wall hangings that won't be washed—just shaken occasionally to remove any dust. The bottom line is this: the decision to prewash or not to prewash is up to you. Whatever you're comfortable doing, do it!

SUPPLIES

Sewing machine. You'll need a sewing machine that sews a good straight stitch. You'll also need a walking foot or darning foot if you're planning to machine quilt.

Take a moment to clean and oil your machine; in fact, get into the practice of cleaning your machine before beginning every project. Cotton is a great fiber, but it does create lint under the feed dogs, which can interfere with the smooth running of your sewing machine.

Rotary-cutting tools. You'll need a rotary cutter, cutting mat, and a clear acrylic ruler. The 6" x 24" ruler works well for cutting long strips and squares. You should also have a large square ruler (such as 9" x 9", 12" x 12", or 15" x 15") for squaring up quilt blocks. In addition, a small Bias Square® ruler comes in handy for cleanup cuts (see step 1 of "Rotary Cutting" below).

Thread. Use a good-quality, all-purpose cotton or cotton-covered polyester thread. Choose a neutral color such as gray, as it won't show through when you're piecing light and dark fabrics together.

Basic sewing tools. You'll need needles for hand and machine sewing, pins, and fabric scissors for cutting threads. Don't forget the seam ripper—the smaller the better so the point can slide through the stitches easily. You'll also need an iron and ironing board for pressing seams.

ROTARY CUTTING

All the projects in this book are designed for quick-and-easy rotary cutting. Here's a quick lesson on rotary how-to.

1. Fold the fabric and match the selvages, aligning the crosswise and lengthwise grains as much as possible. Place the folded edge closest to you on the cutting mat. Align a square ruler along the folded edge of the fabric. Then place a long, straight ruler to the left of the square ruler, just covering the uneven raw edges of the left side of the fabric.

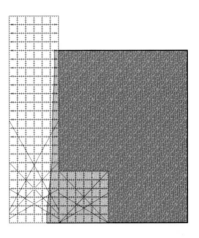

Remove the square ruler and cut along the right edge of the long ruler, rolling the rotary cutter away from you. Discard this cleanup strip. (Reverse this procedure if you're left-handed.)

2. To cut strips, align the required measurement on the ruler with the newly cut edge of the fabric. For example, to cut a 3"-wide strip, place the 3" ruler mark on the edge of the fabric.

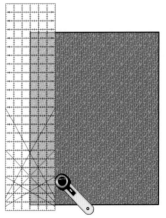

3. To cut squares, cut strips in the required widths. Trim away the selvage ends of the strip. Align the required measurement on the ruler with the left edge of the strip and cut a square. Continue cutting squares until you have the number you need.

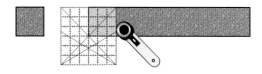

MACHINE PIECING

The most important thing to remember about machine piecing is to maintain a consistent scant ¼"-wide seam allowance. Some sewing machines have a special ¼" foot that measures exactly ¼" from the center needle position to the edge of the foot. This feature allows you to use the edge of the presser foot to guide the fabric for a perfect ¼"-wide seam allowance.

Test your ¼" foot for accuracy. I recently found out my foot was creating a seam allowance larger than a scant ¼" and my blocks and borders weren't matching up properly. The quick fix was to move my sewing-machine needle to the right about the width of three threads, and I was back in business with an accurate seam allowance.

If your machine doesn't have such a foot, create a seam guide by placing the edge of a piece of tape ¼" to the right of the needle.

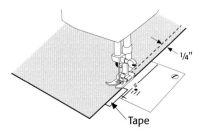

FOLDED-CORNER PIECING

You'll love this technique for sewing half-square triangles to squares and rectangles—without cutting a single triangle piece!

1. Cut the pieces—squares, or squares and rectangles—as instructed in the quilt directions. Draw a diagonal line from corner to corner on the wrong side of each small square.

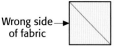

2. Place a marked square right sides together with the rectangle or larger square, aligning the small square with the corner or edge of the larger piece as illustrated in the quilt directions.

3. Sew directly on the drawn line. Trim the excess fabric, leaving a ¼"-wide seam allowance. Press the seams toward the resulting small triangle. Repeat to sew, trim, and press additional squares to the unit as instructed.

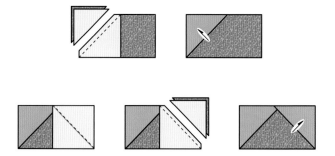

CHAIN PIECING

Chain piecing is an efficient, time-saving system for sewing together multiple like pieces and units.

1. Sew the first pair of pieces from cut edge to cut edge, using about 12 stitches per inch. At the end of the seam, stop sewing, but don't cut the thread.

2. Feed the next pair of pieces under the presser foot, as close as possible to the first pair. Continue feeding pieces through the machine without cutting the thread in between. There is no need to backstitch, since each seam will be crossed and held by another seam.

3. When all pieces have been sewn, remove the chain from the machine and clip the threads between pieces.

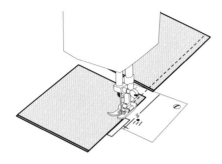

Easing

If two pieces that will be sewn together differ slightly in size (by less than ⅛"), pin the places where the two pieces should match. Next pin in between, if necessary, to distribute the excess fabric evenly. Sew the seam with the longer piece on the bottom, next to the feed dogs. The feed dogs will help ease the two pieces together.

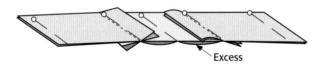
Excess

Pressing

Pressing is very important for many reasons. It helps sink the thread into the fabric, it sets the seam, and it helps you see if the pieces are stitched accurately. Remember that pressing and ironing are two different things. While pressing, use an up-and-down motion and avoid sliding the iron back and forth over a block. This will help prevent distortion. I use both a dry iron and steam, depending on how the fabric reacts to the different types of heat. Make sure the iron face is clean.

The traditional rule in quiltmaking is to press seams to one side, toward the darker color wherever possible. Press the seam flat from the

wrong side first, and then press the seam in the desired direction from the right side. Be particularly careful when pressing bias seams or edges.

When joining two seamed units, plan ahead and press the seam allowances in the opposite directions as shown. This reduces bulk and makes it easier to match seam lines. Where two seams meet, the seam allowances will butt against each other, making it easier to join units with perfectly matched seam intersections.

Opposing seams

Borders

For best results, don't cut border strips and sew them directly to the quilt sides without measuring first, unless the quilt is small—for example, a wall hanging. The edges of a quilt often measure slightly longer than the measurement through the quilt center, due to stretching during construction. For this reason, measure the quilt top through the center in both directions to determine how long to cut the border strips. Then sew the strips to the edges of the quilt, easing to fit. This step ensures that the finished quilt will be as straight and as "square" as possible, without wavy edges.

Plain border strips are cut along the crosswise grain and seamed where extra length is needed.

Straight-Cut Borders

All the borders in this book are either straight-cut borders or have details of one kind or another. For the detailed borders, please follow the directions given with the individual project. For straight-cut borders:

1. Measure the *length* of the quilt top through the center. Cut border strips to that measurement, piecing as necessary; mark the center of the quilt edges and the border strips. Pin the borders to the sides of the quilt top, matching the center marks and ends and easing as necessary. Sew the border strips in place. Press seams toward the border.

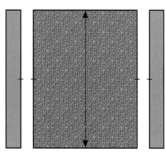

Measure center of quilt,
top to bottom.
Mark centers.

2. Measure the *width* of the quilt top through the center, including the side borders just added. Cut border strips to that measurement, piecing as necessary; mark the center of the quilt edges and the border strips. Pin the borders to the top and bottom edges of the quilt top, matching the center marks and ends and easing as necessary; stitch. Press seams toward the border.

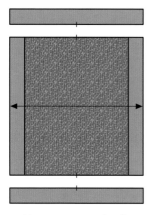

Measure center of quilt,
side to side, including borders.
Mark centers.

MARKING THE QUILTING LINES

Whether or not to mark the quilting designs depends upon the type of quilting you'll be doing. Marking isn't necessary if you plan to quilt in the ditch, outline quilt a uniform distance from seam lines, or free-motion quilt in a random pattern over the quilt surface or in selected areas. For more complex quilting designs, mark the quilt top before the quilt is layered with batting and backing.

Choose a marking tool that will be visible on your fabric and test it on fabric scraps to be sure the marks can be removed easily.

I use blue painter's tape for straight-line quilting. This tape is designed not to leave a sticky residue on your walls—or on your quilt! You can find painter's tape at your local hardware store, and it comes in a variety of widths. By using both edges of the tape you can achieve better speed as well as a great appearance in your quilting.

FINISHING

In talking with quilters, I have discovered that we all have our favorite and least favorite steps in quiltmaking. My love is the design and construction process. I'm still learning to "get into" the finishing process: making the quilt sandwich, deciding what and how to quilt, and so on. Someday I hope to slow down enough to embrace it all. Wish me luck!

LAYERING THE QUILT

The quilt "sandwich" consists of backing, batting, and the quilt top. Cut the quilt backing at least 4" larger in both length and width than the quilt top. For large quilts, it's usually necessary to sew two or three lengths of fabric together to make a backing of the required size. Trim away the selvages before piecing the lengths together. Press seams open to make quilting easier.

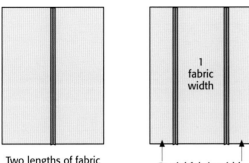

Two lengths of fabric seamed in the center

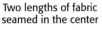
Partial fabric width

Batting comes packaged in standard bed sizes, or it can be purchased by the yard. Several weights or lofts (thicknesses) are available. Thick battings are fine for tied quilts and comforters; a thin batting is better, however, if you intend to quilt by hand or machine.

To put it all together:

1. Spread the backing, wrong side up, on a flat, clean surface. Anchor it with pins or masking tape. Be careful not to stretch the backing out of shape.

2. Center the batting over the backing, smoothing out any wrinkles.

3. Center the pressed quilt top, right side up, on top of the batting. Smooth out any wrinkles and make sure the quilt-top edges are parallel to the edges of the backing.

4. Starting in the center, baste with needle and thread and work diagonally to each corner. Continue basting in a grid of horizontal and vertical lines 6" to 8" apart. Finish by basting around the edges.

NOTE: For machine quilting, you may baste the layers with rustproof safety pins. Place pins about 6" to 8" apart, away from the areas you intend to quilt.

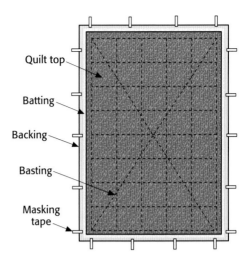

For small projects that I plan to machine quilt, I also have great success using a spray adhesive to anchor the layers together! There are several brands available on the market but my favorite is 505 Spray, which doesn't have toxic fumes and works very well.

MACHINE QUILTING

Machine quilting is suitable for all types of quilts, from crib to full-sized bed quilts. With machine quilting, you can quickly complete quilts and start the next project that is calling out to you.

1. For straight-line quilting, it's extremely helpful to have a walking foot to help feed the quilt layers through the machine without the layers shifting or puckering. Some machines have a built-in walking foot; other machines require a separate attachment.

Walking foot

Quilting in the ditch

Outline quilting

2. For free-motion quilting, you need a darning foot and the ability to drop the feed dogs on your machine. With free-motion quilting, you don't turn the fabric under the needle but instead guide the fabric in the direction of the design. Use free-motion quilting to outline quilt a fabric motif or to create stippling or other curved designs.

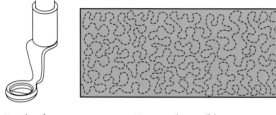

Darning foot   Free-motion quilting

BINDING

Bindings can be made from straight-grain or bias-grain strips of fabric. All of the quilts in this book call for a French double-fold (straight-grain) binding.

To cut straight-grain binding strips, cut 2½"-wide strips across the width of the fabric. You'll need enough strips to go around the perimeter of the quilt plus 10" for seams and mitered-corner folds.

1. With right sides together, place strips at right angles and stitch across the corner as shown. Trim excess fabric and press the seams open.

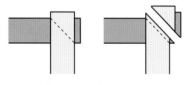

Joining straight-cut strips

2. Fold the strip in half lengthwise, wrong sides together, and press. Unfold one end and trim at a 45° angle, turn under ¼", and press. Turning the end under at an angle distributes the bulk so

you won't have a lump where the two ends of the binding meet.

Fold line

3. Trim the batting and backing even with the quilt top. If you plan to add a hanging sleeve, do so now before attaching the binding (see page 79).

4. Starting on one side of the quilt, with right sides together and using a ¼"-wide seam allowance, stitch the binding to the quilt, keeping the raw edges even with the quilt-top edge. Start the stitching a few inches from the start of the binding and end the stitching ¼" from the corner of the quilt with a backstitch. Clip the thread.

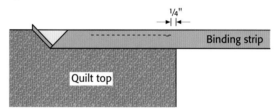

¼"

Binding strip

Quilt top

5. Turn the quilt so that you'll be stitching down the next side. Fold the binding up, away from the quilt, and then back down onto itself, parallel with the edge of the quilt top. Begin stitching at the edge, backstitching to secure. Repeat on the remaining edges and corners of the quilt.

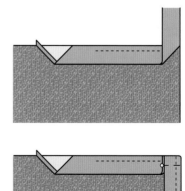

6. When you reach the beginning of the binding, stop sewing and overlap the beginning stitches by 2" with the binding tail. Cut away any excess binding, trimming the end at a 45° angle. Tuck the end of the binding into the fold and finish the seam.

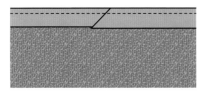

7. Fold the binding over the raw edges of the quilt to the back, with the folded edge covering the row of machine stitching, and blindstitch in place. A miter will form at each corner. Blindstitch the mitered corners.

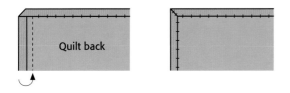

Quilt back

ADDING A SLEEVE

If you plan to display your finished quilt on the wall, be sure to add a hanging sleeve to hold the rod.

1. Using leftover fabric from the quilt or a piece of muslin, cut a strip 6" to 8" wide and 1" shorter than the width of the quilt at the top edge. Fold the ends of the strip under ½" and then ½" again; stitch.

2. Fold the strip in half lengthwise, wrong sides together; center and baste the raw edges to the top edge of the quilt back. The top edge of the

sleeve will be secured when the binding is sewn on the quilt.

Baste sleeve to top edge of quilt.

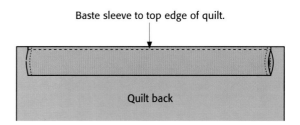

Quilt back

3. Finish the sleeve after the binding has been attached by blindstitching the bottom of the sleeve in place. Push the bottom edge of the sleeve up just a bit to provide a little give so the hanging rod doesn't put strain on the quilt itself.

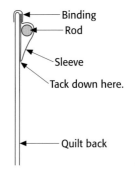

Binding
Rod
Sleeve
Tack down here.
Quilt back

SIGNING YOUR QUILT

Be sure to sign and date your quilt. Future generations will be interested to know more than just who made it and when. Labels can be as elaborate or as simple as you desire. The information can be handwritten, typed, or embroidered. Be sure to include the name of the quilt, your name, your city and state, the date, the name of the recipient if it's a gift, and any other interesting or important information about the quilt.

About the Author

This is Terry Martin's fifth quilting book, and she has many more ideas than time. She loves to lecture and teach classes, and she hopes eventually to translate more of her quilting ideas into books.

Terry lives with a very understanding husband and daughter in Snohomish, Washington. She is active in her quilting community as a member of the Busy Bee Quilt Guild of Snohomish and as a teacher in local shops and on quilting cruises to Alaska. She is always willing to head off for a weekend of quilting at a local retreat. She loves the friendship, support, and never-ending laughter that her quilting friends provide her.

Acknowledgments

It takes a village to do most things, and creating a quilt book is no exception. I wish to thank Robert Kaufman Fabrics for providing fabulous fabric with only a week's notice.

A huge thank-you and hug for my machine quilters, Barb Dau and Becky Marshall. They always add that extra dimension to my work.

And thank you, Martingale & Company, for taking my scratchings (the proverbial ugly duckling) and turning them into this swan.